RAISING

Identical

TWINS

RAISING
Identical
TWINS

THE UNIQUE CHALLENGES AND
JOYS OF THE EARLY YEARS

LORI DUFFY FOSTER

ISBN: 978-0-692-93464-7
Library of Congress Control Number: 2017953092

Edited by Richard Sullivan
Cover image and author image by Bridget Reed, www.bridgetreed.com
Cover concept by Riley Foster
Cover Design by Fiona Jayde Media
Interior Design by The Deliberate Page

Printed and bound in USA
First printing: September 2017

Published by Austinburg Road Publications
austinburgroadpublications@gmail.com

Visit www.loriduffyfoster.com

For Jonathan and Matthew, our bonus babies who forever changed our lives in ways we could never have imagined and would never in a million years change. Our hearts have grown because of you. We never knew there was so much love in the world to give and to receive.

For Riley and Kiersten, who have shown amazing amounts of patience with their twin siblings and with their sometime-crazed parents over the years. Your lives changed dramatically when Matthew and Jonathan were born, but you embraced them and became the best role models we could ask for. We love you and we are so proud of the adults you are becoming.

For my husband Tom, who encouraged me to write the blog that is the basis of this book, and has always been there for me with his love and support. You get me and that is one of the many things I love about you.

TABLE OF CONTENTS

INTRODUCTION

Throughout my pregnancy, we were told our twins were definitely fraternal. Their placentas were on opposite sides of the uterus. Though identical twins can have their own placentas, they generally implant close together, my obstetrician said.

Then, early one morning in January, 2007, exactly thirty-seven weeks into my pregnancy, Matthew and Jonathan were born, and the pediatrician congratulated us on our identical boys. DNA tests confirmed it, as did our own confusion over who was who. I was terrified. I had heard so many myths and misconceptions about identical twins. What if we did everything wrong? Was there some secret to raising identical twins? Was there really any difference at all between raising identicals and fraternals?

I searched for information on the things that make identical twins different from their fraternal peers. I found plenty of scientific information, but not the stuff I craved. I wanted to know whether they would walk and talk at the same time, whether they would like the same foods, whether to dress them alike, whether we should keep them together in school. I wanted to know how to raise them so each had his own identity, but also cherished and appreciated the bond between them.

My frustration with the lack of information led to the creation of a blog, *The Boys: Raising Identical Twins* (twinsblog.troupsburg.com). I wrote about my own experiences, joys and frustrations in raising Matthew and Jonathan. I explored challenges, dynamics and answers. The response was incredible. Immediately, I began receiving emails from people who were grateful, so grateful, to finally find information that pertained specifically to their situations. Most were parents of identical twins, but many were identical twins themselves.

When our boys turned six, I decided to quit posting out of respect for their privacy. Still, the page views mounted and the emails continued. New parents were finding the blog. It remained one of the few resources out there.

Given the interest, I wanted to expand on what I'd written in the past and make the information available to more people, make something parents and twins could share and pass on. So I decided to create this book, which is based on the blog. *Raising Identical Twins: The Unique Challenges and Joys of the Early Years* is not a reference guide, a discipline manual or some kind of philosophy on raising children. Rather, it is a compilation of my own experiences and observations coupled with research and analysis, written in hopes of taking some of the stress out of identical-twin parenthood for others.

So often I've heard people argue that raising identical twins is no different than raising fraternal twins. In reality, that's not true. Raising two people who look alike, are the same age and share identical brain waves is a challenge of its own. Though the challenge can be frustrating at times, it is most often unbearably rewarding. My hope is that parents who read this book will find reassurance in our experiences with Jonathan and Matthew, and will enter identical-twin parenthood with nothing but confidence and anticipation.

PART 1

Look-A-Like Babies

(Ages 0 to one year)

The moment I learned our twins were identical was both terrifying and exciting. I was excited for the obvious reasons, for the same reasons most people are intrigued by two tiny human beings who share so many physical features and personality traits. Raising identical twins is a privilege. It has given me a front-row seat and a backstage pass from which to observe one of the greatest bonds possible between two human beings. But the terror sometimes overwhelmed the excitement, especially in that first year. I was not a first-time mother, so I had experience on my side, but I worried often about confusing their identities, being unable to feed and bathe two babies at once, bonding with two tiny souls knowing I would have little time alone with either one—all things I had to face before I would know whether I was capable of achieving them.

The first year was hard. I won't lie. But it was also beautiful, and it flew by quickly. To emerge whole from the experience, it is important not to lose yourself in the chaos. You have an identity to preserve as well. So as you enter identical-twin parenthood, I suggest you develop tools that will help you feel connected, rested, whole and healthy. Little things can make a huge difference. With a husband who traveled frequently, I craved adult interaction after our twins were born. So, while I nursed, I telephoned friends who were also at home with young children. I kept a novel on each level of the house I could pick up while nursing or whenever the twins were otherwise occupied for a few moments. The novels helped keep my mind sharp and fueled my passion for fiction. I hired a nanny once a week so I could take the older kids somewhere special on their own, just like old times, easing some of the guilt I felt about all the time that caring for the twins took away from them. And unlike many new twin moms I had come to know, I left the house with my little guys in tow starting when they were just a few days old. The outings were crucial for all three of us. They gave me incentive to shower, dress decently and interact with others. They gave the babies all kids of helpful stimulation.

If I could go back in time, I would have carved out time to exercise more. I would have met with friends sans kids now and then, napped when the twins did rather than worrying about housework, and eaten a healthier diet. Keep in mind as you embark on this journey that a happy, healthy parent is a good parent. Caring for yourself should not be considered selfish or a luxury. It should be a priority. Congratulations and enjoy the ride!

THEY'RE HERE! NOW HOW DO WE TELL THEM APART?

The first few weeks

My husband and I had a problem, a serious problem. We were expecting fraternal twins, babies who looked like brothers, but who had their own identifying physical characteristics. One would be smaller, have different hair, a rounded head, something, anything that would help us tell them apart. We had nothing but the hospital-issued bracelets on their wrists. Matthew and Jonathan were slightly different in weight at birth, but only slightly. One was born at six pounds and nine ounces, the other at six pounds and two ounces. The difference in their weights was not great enough to be helpful.

More than two thirds of identical twins share placentas, often leaving one twin deprived of nutrients and, therefore, noticeably smaller at birth. Not so with Matthew and Jonathan. Theirs was the safest type of twin pregnancy (two placentas and two sacs) and the most likely to produce the most identical of twins. We didn't dare identify them by colored-coded clothing. What if we forgot who was who when they were naked and bathing? We feared ID bracelets or anklets would break or fall off. Tattooing was out of the question. It would have been unethical and illegal.

We kept their bracelets on for a week while we thought about our dilemma. Finally, I bought a bottle of dark blue nail polish. Then I closed my eyes and pointed. Jonathan was the winner. I didn't dare paint his fingernails for fear he would chew the polish off and swallow it. So I chose his toenails. Not one of them, but all five on one foot. I wasn't about to take chances. So that's how Jonathan begins this life—with pretty blue toenails.

COMMONLY USED METHODS FOR DIFFERENTIATING BETWEEN IDENTICAL TWINS

Certain people reacted with near-horror when they saw the polish on Jonathan's toenails. For them, nail polish on a boy was incomprehensible, even on a baby and even in a boyish hue. If your babies are not readily distinguishable from one another at birth and you cringe at the idea of polish, don't fret. There are many ways to set twins apart. Settle on the method that works best for you. Whatever method you choose is not permanent. The day will come when you no longer need it.

Here are few suggestions I've collected over the years in talking with other parents of identical twins:

Identification bracelets/anklets: You can make your own or scour the Internet, where you will find plenty of personalized jewelry designed specifically for babies. Just make sure nothing on the jewelry presents a choking hazard or might be toxic if chewed.

Color-coded clothing: This method is especially helpful when you can tell your babies apart, but others have more trouble. It can become expensive, however, when you have to shop for outfits only in certain colors and it can be confusing for those who rely on the method if you run out of clean, appropriately weighted clothes in one twin's assigned color.

Permanent marker: With permanent marker, you can put an initial or some other identifying mark somewhere on the body of one baby. Most people choose the feet. Like the nail polish, it should be reapplied as it starts to fade.

LATCHING AT LAST
The first few weeks

I'm tired. So very tired.

Matthew and Jonathan sucked on their tongues inside the womb. So when they emerged, they had already developed their first bad habits. They persistently lifted their tongues to the roofs of their mouths instead of accepting a breast or a bottle nipple on top of their tongues. The habit made it impossible to nurse them and difficult to bottle feed them. So I found myself first trying to nurse each twin separately; then bottling feeding both; then pumping.

It has been exhausting, especially since their feedings are less than three hours apart at this age. But today, on their tenth day of life, something beautiful happened. My efforts and persistence paid off. Both boys latched during the same feeding, and both boys nursed like champions.

NURSING TWINS

Some people will insist breastfeeding twins is impossible. They will discourage new mothers from even trying. Cover your ears. It is not impossible. Nursing two simply takes practice along with lots of trial and error, not unlike nursing a singleton for the first time. It also will save you a ton of money. I didn't realize just how much I had saved nursing until I switched to formula.

Here are a few tips and tidbits that might help if you plan to give it a try:

Supplementing with a bottle now and then will not destroy their abilities to nurse.

That is a myth, propagated by those who are breastfeeding purists. My boys had a blood condition that could have resulted in high bilirubin levels weeks after birth, rather than days. Because of that, our pediatrician recommended two ounces of formula each day for a month. Once the boys latched to nurse, nothing stopped them, certainly not a tiny bottle of formula once a day. They easily converted to exclusive breastfeeding when the one-month term had passed.

My sister exclusively nursed her children when she was on maternity leave, but then switched to formula during day-care hours. She successfully nursed her children morning and night for several more months. I have talked to many, many mothers over the years who have successfully combined breastfeeding and formula feeding. A little bit of breast milk is better than none. So, if you are unable to nurse full time or want to breastfeed for only a few days, weeks or months, do not let anyone tell you shouldn't bother.

Do remember, though, that production depends on demand. If you cut back on breastfeeding, your breasts will reduce the amount they produce. So if you supplement often, try to do so on a regular schedule. If you cut down for a while and want to increase production, an extra pumping a day can be helpful.

If you chose to formula feed exclusively, ignore the judgments.
A happy mother is a good mother and if nursing brings you down physically or mentally, don't do it. Breast is best, but formula is pretty darned good, too. Only you can decide what is best for you and your family. Your decision is no one's business but your own.

Tandem Feeding is awesome if you can do it.
Some people are so good at this, and I envy them. They just grab a nursing pillow, pop a twin on each side and let them go to town. Twenty minutes later, they are done. Both babies are happy and drunk on their mommy's milk. No twin screaming from hunger while the other sucks it down. No mommy guilt for making one twin wait.

Though I managed to feed both my boys at once about a dozen times, I was pretty much a failure at tandem nursing. I am larger breasted and those things just fell all over the place, making it difficult to nurse without supporting my breast with one hand. I could have tried harder. Instead, I resorted to "Baby Einstein." I'd pop in the DVD and set one twin in front of it in a bouncy seat. The thrill of the video overwhelmed the gnawing hunger each time, allowing me to nurse each boy in peace.

I know. I know. One-month-olds shouldn't have screen time, but sometimes you just have to do what you have to do.

Help in nursing twins is at your fingertips.
If you are nervous about breastfeeding twins, go online and search "nursing twins." The amount of information available is overwhelming.

You can read instructions, watch videos and chat with others who are nursing twins individually and in tandem. My favorite book on breastfeeding in general is *The Nursing Mother's Companion* by Kathleen Huggins. Her book includes information on nursing multiples, weaning from breast milk, resuming breastfeeding after a break, nursing after a c-section, methods for increasing production, introducing solids, everything you can think of. I relied on her book for all four of my children.

IDENTICAL TWINNING:
MISCONCEPTIONS & MISINFORMATION

The first two months

At my first follow-up appointment after I delivered the twins, I told my obstetrician what the hospital pediatrician had said, that Jonathan and Matthew were identical. Let's check, he suggested, and he pulled up the results of a hospital test on his computer. Definitely fraternal, he said, adding that sometimes, twins are born looking alike, but they differentiate as the days go by. My husband and I were puzzled, and so was our pediatrician. The boys looked alike, they had the same blood type, they started latching to nurse at the same feeding on the same day, they slept, pooped and ate on the same schedule. Everything about them screamed "identical." Yet, my OB was an expert, wasn't he?

The hospital wouldn't lie, would it?

Six weeks later, we still couldn't tell them apart and I couldn't take it anymore. Honestly, my inability to immediately differentiate between them was making me feel like a failure. It shouldn't have, but it did. Our pediatrician suggested we have the twins DNA tested, something that is not covered by insurance but is much more affordable these days with improvements in technology. So we had them tested through Proactive Genetics, a reputable and highly recommended company.

It was easy. We received a kit in the mail for less than two hundred dollars and rubbed large swabs gently inside their cheeks and ours. We put the swabs in the test tubes the lab provided and mailed them off in the box the company gave us. The results were supposed to take three weeks. Ours took only one week via email. They were, according to the company, identical.

When I told my OB about the results, he suggested the hospital's mistake was just a fluke and one he hadn't questioned given the placement of our twins in utero. Their placentas were on opposite sides of the uterus. In the few cases he'd seen where twins like ours were identical, the placentas were side-by-side. At my insistence, we took a closer look at the hospital's test.

This is what we found:

The hospital where I gave birth to our twins, like many around the country, does not do DNA testing. Technicians simply conduct physical tests of the placentas. They study them to determine whether they are two fused placentas, or one shared placenta. That's it. DNA has nothing to do with it. In our case, that was a no-brainer. Matthew and Jonathan each had clearly distinct placentas. From that result, the lab tech wrongly and irresponsibly concluded the boys were fraternal. And that's what appeared on my OB's computer screen.

Over and over again, I hear of twin parents who are told their twins are fraternal, but who still simply cannot tell their twins apart. They post photos of their twins on online bulletin boards, hoping for answers. Like us, those parents are told the placentas were tested at the hospital. "The babies can't be identical: Just look at the results," the doctors say.

The parents scratch their heads and try to persuade themselves the hospitals and the doctors must be right. But most every one of those parents I met online later learned through DNA testing their instincts were correct. Their twins (and sometimes two of their triplets) were indeed identical despite the protests of their OBs. In fact, we now know about one third of identical twins have separate placentas and sacs.

I'm not sure why some OBs and hospitals still subscribe to the idea that two placentas equal fraternal twins, and continue to disseminate that misinformation to their patients. A quick Internet search will immediately prove them wrong, so it's not as if the information is some highly guarded secret or some off-the-wall theory. I can only suppose their ignorance stems from the fact that zygosity (the type of twinning) is irrelevant in determining neonatal risk factors for twins and their moms. What matters from a healthcare perspective is simply whether they share placentas and/or sacs, not whether they share DNA.

Still, doctors and hospital staff have an ethical responsibility to stay current in their fields, or to at least defer to others if they are unsure. My OB should have known better. The hospital technician should have known better. It is time for change.

TYPES OF TWINS

Fraternal (dizygotic twins): This is the easiest type of twinning to explain. Fraternal twinning occurs when a woman drops more than one egg during a cycle and both eggs are fertilized. The tendency to release more than one egg can be an inherited condition or the result of fertility medicines. The babies can implant anywhere in the uterus, though sometimes they implant so close together that the placentas fuse and might appear as one.

Physical or biological differences are often enough to confirm they are fraternal. Fraternal twins share no more DNA than any other siblings. They might be of different genders, have different blood types or be obviously different in physical ways such as hair color, eye color or body type. If, as in our case, parents can find no significant biological or physical differences, it is possible the babies are identical. Only a DNA test can confirm whether they are identical or fraternal.

Identical (monozygotic) twins: Identical twins form when a fertilized egg splits and becomes two separate human beings, who shared the same DNA. Researchers are unsure what causes the split. Some evidence exists to show it is triggered by a combination of an inherited enzyme in the sperm and a weakness in the egg shell, but the verdict is still out. Others scientists still believe it is a random occurrence.

There are three different types of identical twins: those who have their own placentas and sacs; those who share a placenta, but have their own sacs; and those who share both a placenta and a sac. Let's look at each one.

- *Dizygotic/dizygotic twins* (individual placentas, individual sacs): Until recently, most doctors assumed all di/di twins were fraternal. Advances in DNA testing have proven that theory false. We now know, without a doubt, at least one-fourth and, possibly, up to one-third or all di/di pregnancies produce identical twins. According to the Twin to Twin Transfusion Syndrome (TTTS) Foundation, this type of identical twinning occurs when the egg splits within four days of fertilization, long before the newly formed eggs fall into the uterus.

- *Monozygotic/dizygotic twins* (shared placentas, individual sacs): These twins develop when the split occurs within about a week of fertilization, according to the TTTS Foundation's website. The eggs implant together and form one placenta. In most cases, the common placenta is not a problem. The babies develop normally and the pregnancy is no more eventful than any other twin pregnancy. But sometimes a significant imbalance develops and one baby gets more nutrients than the other. This is called twin-to-twin transfusion syndrome, a dangerous and, sometimes, life-threatening condition. Early detection through constant monitoring can prevent defects and save lives.

- *Monozygotic/monozygotic* (shared placenta, shared sac): This is the most risky twin pregnancy, occurring when the split comes later, about nine days or more after fertilization, the TTTS Foundation notes. Along with the possibility of TTS, doctors must be on the lookout for tangled or compressed umbilical cords. But, with constant monitoring, the odds of a safe and healthy delivery are good. A friend of mine carried identical triplets who shared a sac more than thirty weeks and all three girls were born healthy.

IT'S ALL RELATIVE

Three months

I am tired. I am stressed. But I am so grateful.

With my husband traveling frequently and my social life limited by two infants, a five-year-old daughter and a six-year-old son, I find myself seeking adult interaction online with people who understand my situation: other parents of twins. Their shared experiences have helped me realize how fortunate I am in terms of my own health and sanity to have birthed healthy, full-term identical twins as opposed to any other type of twin with health issues or differing biological clocks.

My guys sleep, eat and even poop on the same schedule. No significant variations so far and they are three months old. I still get next-to-no sleep as I attempt to nurse while also taking the older kids back and forth to school, transporting them to various activities, keeping up with their homework, running errands, cleaning the house and providing meals, but I can't even begin to imagine how difficult my life would be if one twin were colicky or one habitually rose early and fell asleep early while other did the opposite.

If I change one baby, I know the other needs changing, too. If I feed one, I know the other is hungry as well. When one naps or crashes for the night, I know the other will, too. No staying up late with one while getting up early with the other. No feeding one only to feed the other an hour later. No continuous diaper changes.

I salute those parents. Compared to them, I have it easy.

IDENTICAL TWINS AND BIOLOGICAL CLOCKS

I have found no studies that focus on when healthy identical twins sleep, poop, pee and crave food, but I've asked a lot of parents about their experiences. Most have shared similar observations, that when one twin dirties a diaper, the other will dirty his ten minutes later; or that both twins become sleepy around the same time. All this can change, of course, with a cold or the flu or a bad dream that keeps one twin up all night, but the theory seems to have some credibility. I'm sure some of these biological similarities will change over time thanks to environmental influences, but my twins are ten years old as I write this, and their biological clocks are still very similar.

SEPARATE CRIBS
Four months

Since birth, Jonathan and Matthew have shared a crib. It made sense to us, given their proximity in the womb. They snuggled together for nearly nine months. Why not make the transition to the outside world easier by putting them together? They seem to appreciate and need each other. If we put them down on opposite sides of the crib, walk away and come back a few minutes later, we'll find them both in the center of the crib fast asleep with their heads touching. It happens every time.

So it is with sadness that we separate them now at four months old. But it is time. Matthew and Jonathan are getting bigger and, when they roll over, they swing their arms, punching each other and waking each other. (We're hoping that's not an indicator of battles to come!) It was hard, but a few days ago, we placed their cribs side-by-side so they can reach through the spaces in the rails and touch each other. And that's how I found them last night. Each had his body pressed against the rails so they were nearly touching in much the same way as they touched heads in their shared crib. They were fast asleep.

SHOULD TWINS SHARE A CRIB?

Opinions on whether infant twins should sleep together vary with some experts saying shared cribs are dangerous and others declaring them necessary to healthy development. These days, many hospitals place twins in one crib, insisting co-sleeping makes the transition from the womb easier. Our boys slept together in an oversized hospital crib from birth. If you decide to place your babies together at night or for naps, keep safety and your sanity in mind. It makes sense to separate twins when they become more mobile, bumping into each other and waking each other up.

GOOD-BYE BLUE NAIL POLISH!

Four months

We're celebrating. The bottle is in the trash and Jonathan is finally free of the artificial marker of difference. A few weeks ago, just after their four-month birthday, we notice blue veins forming across the bridges of their noses. Jonathan's was thick while Matthew's was thin. We didn't dare rely on them immediately though. What if they changed and became indistinguishable again? But we've been playing the guessing game for weeks now, testing ourselves to see whether the vein system is reliable, and, so far, it is. My confidence does not come entirely from the vein formation, however. Physical and personality differences are beginning to emerge. Jonathan is slightly weaker and more laid back than his twin brother. If I mix them up, I can now tell who is who after a few minutes of observation. It's a good feeling as their mom. A very good feeling.

MIXED UP YOUR TWINS?

Maybe Microsoft can help. Chris Griffith, a reporter for *The Australian*, tested Microsoft's new facial recognition software with the help of six sets of identical twins. The camera was not fooled, he wrote in his Aug. 20, 2015, article. The software easily distinguished between the most identical of siblings.

SHARING THE LOVIE
Four months

Each of our older kids grew up with "lovies," plush animals they slept with at night beginning at birth. So when we learned nearly twenty-one weeks through my pregnancy that I was carrying twins, the older kids and I set out to find lovies for their brothers. We settled on a yellow bear for Matthew and a blue puppy for Jonathan. They were the same brand and the same size. As far as we could tell, they had the same feel. We did not place them in their cribs immediately as we did with the other kids. Jonathan and Matthew were smaller than their siblings due to their slightly early arrivals, and they shared a crib. They had each other for comfort.

But when we separated them at four months, we decide it was time. The plushies went to bed with them at night and during naps. After a few weeks, they began hanging out with Matthew and Jonathan on the play mat or in the bouncy seats as well. That's when the problems began, when the plushies were on the floor within reach of both twins. Jonathan routinely ignored his blue puppy and lunged for the yellow bear, which Matthew protected fiercely. Come bedtime or naptime, Jonathan shunned his blue puppy, reaching through the crib rails for Matthew's yellow bear. Finally, we caved. As I write, both boys are fast asleep in their cribs, each with a yellow bear tucked under his arm.

UNIQUE APPROACHES, IDENTICAL RESULTS

Nine months

Physically, Matthew and Jonathan are almost indistinguishable. They are the same height, they have the same head circumference and their weights are always within a few ounces of each other. The only way we can tell them apart in photos is by the vein across their noses: Matthew's is narrow and Jonathan's is thick. Their personalities, however, couldn't be more different. It started ten days after birth, when they finally caught on to the whole concept of nursing. Matthew would latch instantly, suck furiously for five minutes and then quit. Jonathan could take up to ten minutes to latch. But I'd have to pull him off forty minutes later. The differences only grew from there.

Now, at nine months, Matthew easily pulls himself up on the coffee table, bridges the gap to the sofa, edges quickly along and grabs a stuffed animal he'd been eying. Then he drops his butt to the floor with the animal in his hands (and in his mouth). Jonathan sits in the center of the living room watching. In the stroller, as we go for walks or hurry through the grocery store, Matthew leans forward, yanking on the bar in front of him and trying to lift his body out. Jonathan leans back and rests his feet on the bar. He observes the world around him with a quiet grin on his face.

But we've learned not to underestimate Jonathan. He observed for months as Matthew struggled to roll to his side, then to his tummy and then back again. He was still not rolling at nearly seven months old and we were concerned. He was barely lifting his head off the floor. So we called the pediatrician. That day, he started rolling everywhere and quickly caught up to his twin. He applied the same technique to crawling. He watched Matthew perfect the combat crawl; then the hands-and-knees crawl; then work his way from crawling to sitting. Once Matthew got it all figured out, Jonathan dove in.

It took Jonathan about two days to accomplish what had taken Matthew several weeks. So, as I watch Matthew pull up once more with his eyes on a cup that his older sister had left on the table, I am not concerned. I know Jonathan is watching with me, and that one day soon he will surprise his brother by beating him to the object of his quest.

WHEN MILESTONES ARE OUT OF REACH

Identical twins should reach their milestones at about the same age, but premature birth can push those milestones back further than their peers. That's why doctors refer to the "adjusted age" of premature babies. They evaluate preemies with their original birthdates in mind, cutting them some slack for their early entries into this world.

If you suspect your twins are too far behind their adjusted ages, or if one twin lags significantly behind the other, ask your doctor to refer them for evaluations. Each state has its own version of a federally funded program designed to identify children with development delays as soon as possible, from birth to age three. Evaluations through the programs, which are usually administered on a county level, are free.

A LANGUAGE OF THEIR OWN

Nine months

It was just before six this morning when the boys awoke. I was tired. I fed them each a bottle and crawled back into bed, hoping my husband and I could steal just a little more sleep before getting the older kids off to school. Then the growling began—a deep, low, intense guttural growling. It rose from the study we had converted into a nursery and over the railing of the loft, seeping through our bedroom door. It grew louder and stronger and soon was followed by screeching and peals of laughter.

Matthew and Jonathan were chatting and nobody was going to sleep through it. My husband gave up. He rose from bed and went downstairs to free them from their cribs. I knew what he would find. Matthew would be standing where the cribs meet in an L-shape. Jonathan would be sitting, looking up at him. They would burst into fits of laughter and giggles when he walked through the door, just as they have done for the past several months.

We have heard this same conversation with different inflections since they were about four months old. Jonathan and Matthew regularly exchange grins and giggles after sips from their sippy cups. They crawl to each other and position themselves almost head-to-head, growling, laughing and squealing while they try not to fall. They once chatted for thirty minutes while one bounced in the Exersaucer and the other sat on the floor. Part of me is jealous of the secret language they share, but mostly, I'm simply in awe.

TWIN TALK: IS IT FOR REAL?

You've probably seen the adorable YouTube video of the toddling identical twins chatting back and forth in what appears to be a language only they understand. Cryptophasia, or "twin language," is a common development in identical twins. It is cute, but you might not want to encourage it. Researchers believe cryptophasia develops when twins pick up each other's mispronunciations. The result is that they understand each other, but no one else understands either of them. According to a 1998 Oxford University study, the development of a secret language can impair normal language development. This can be a source of frustration and meltdowns in the preschool years.

A MOMENT OF TERROR: JONNY'S FALL

Nine months

I find myself watching Jonathan's every move these days. I watch his expressions, his hand movements, his eyes. I worry when he cries too much, when he seems too tired or too irritable. I look for anything that might indicate he has a brain injury. So far, he seems fine. More than fine. He has caught up to his brother and he is pulling up on everything. He is trying to let go and stand on his own. He is crawling fast. So fast, that he crawled to the slightly cracked-open basement door and fell down twelve stairs two days ago.

It was my fault.

I was distracted.

I had just torn down a book display at the elementary school and had hauled the books into our basement. I was rushing to get the older kids a snack before I had to get my daughter off to dance. I remembered something I had to tell my husband. I got on the phone. A minute or two later, I heard a thud. I had left the door ajar. I threw the phone and found Jonathan on the carpeted wooden landing, sprawled on his tummy. That is an image I will never forget. He was crying when I got to him. That was a good sign. I cradled him and cuddled him, but after five minutes he wanted nothing more to do with that. He had spotted a toy he wanted and Matthew was after it, too. He wriggled out of my lap and played. I called the doctor. Her nurse gave me the symptoms to watch for over the next twenty-four hours. It has been two days and I am still watching.

It was a wake-up call for me.

I had started selling children's books because I felt guilty that I was not making any money. We were finally getting somewhere with our debts when the twins came along. Now, we spend seventy-five dollars a week on formula (I quit nursing after four months.) and another thirty to forty dollars on diapers. I order pizza more often than I should because I don't have time to cook. I've had to buy new clothes because I still haven't lost the baby weight.

But Jonny's accident changed my perspective.

In less than three months, the babies will be drinking milk. In two years, they will be out of diapers (I hope!). I'll lose the weight in time. I can make almost the same amount of money writing articles on my own deadlines, querying them and freelancing them. I've started working on a nonfiction book project that I had abandoned long ago. It involves lots of interviews that I can do at night. I love to interview people. I love to write. Writing relieves my stress. Selling books only added to it.

I can't blame Jonny's accident on my job. There will always be distractions. It was one of many. But I can try to lessen the stress. I can try to take care of myself so that I can take care of them. The children's books I sold were great. I love them. I don't mind pushing them on people even though I generally dislike doing any kind of sales. But success involves a lot of marketing, a lot of lugging boxes around and a lot of coordination with other people. It was always on my mind. With infant twins and two older children whose world has recently been turned upside down, I have other priorities. I can't afford that kind of distraction. I can't afford to accidentally leave the basement door open again.

THE RACE TO THE GUM LINE

Ten months

The boys' shirts are dripping wet. They are shoving wooden puzzle pieces in their mouths like they haven't eaten in weeks. They are waking up in the middle of the night. They are biting my shoulders, my knees and even my cheeks. They are teething again.

With the appearance of their first teeth at eight months old came the answer to one of the questions about identical twins that had nagged me. Identical twins, I learned, do not cut teeth at the same time. Well, not really. They kind of do, but really they don't. Sort of.

Here's what I mean:

Jonathan got his first tooth ten days before Matthew, but they both got the same two teeth within the same amount of time. Now it is a race for the next set of teeth. Both have started drooling and biting again. Both are waking once during the night, though it seems Jonathan is having a harder time falling back to sleep than Matthew. Both are chewing on their bottle nipples. I am guessing Jonathan will be first, since his teeth emerged before Matthew's during the last round. But I can't be sure.

These guys like to mess with me. They pull me in by differentiating—developing their own ways of doing things, their own gestures, their own preferences. Then, just when I start bragging about how well I can tell my identical twins apart, they pull a switch on me. One starts behaving like the other. I'm betting on Jonathan, but maybe Matthew will surprise me. The important thing is that they both reach the finish line.

And fast, for my sake as much as theirs.

NOT SO IDENTICAL TEETH

Did you know identical twins leave different bite marks? According to a study published in September of 1982 in the Journal of the American Dental Association, the arch formed by the teeth of identical twins is unique to each member of the pair. So are the positions of the teeth themselves. For example, one twin might have an incisor that turns slightly to the right while the same tooth on the other twin twists to the left. Even more interesting is that their bites sometimes mirrored each other's. Researchers came to their conclusions by comparing bite marks of several sets of identical twins.

ATTACK!

Ten months

Previously, I wrote that we were not worried about Jonathan catching up with his brother. He has, and it's payback time. In the old days, when Matthew was mobile and Jonathan refused to wander beyond a two-foot radius, Jonathan would watch with dread as Matthew crawled up to him, grabbed his shirt and started climbing. I knew the cry. I would look over and find Jonathan with his head crushed to his knees and his brother standing triumphantly over him.

A few days ago, I heard that familiar wail and ran over to pull them apart once again. I was surprised to find that Jonathan was not the crier. He was the victor and his brother had trained him well. He is persistent and stubborn and I get nothing done.

I can see it coming. Jonathan gets a gleeful look on his face, and then he takes off. I separate them and he goes after Matthew again. I place them on opposite sides of the room and he's grabbing Matthew's shirt before I can climb over the gate to get back to the dishes I was washing. He has his eyes fixed on Matthew and he will not give up until he has succeeded.

At first, Matthew was so surprised by his brother that he seemed unable to protect himself. Even that has changed. Yesterday, I found them wrestling. Each was trying to pull up on the other. They were grabbing heads and ears and shirts and noses. Then they both fell onto their backs and cried. But while Matthew rubbed his eyes and comforted himself, Jonathan saw an opportunity. He recovered instantly and was back on his hands and knees, heading for his brother with the grin in place once again.

Yes, Matthew has trained him.

Matthew has trained him well.

ALL THAT WRESTLING COULD PAY OFF

Identical twins Brianna Monique Danielson and Nicole Garcia-Colace make their living in the ring with World Wrestling Entertainment. Known as the Bella Twins, both are former WWE Divas Champions.

BONDING WITH TWO

Ten months

When our oldest was a baby, I nursed him back to sleep each time he awoke. Later, when he switched to formula, I gave him a bottle and rocked him. Finally, our pediatrician said he would sleep through the night if we'd just kick the bottle habit. We did and he slept, and I learned that for occasional awakenings, all he needed was soft caresses on his back.

Our daughter didn't like to be cuddled. She still doesn't unless it's on her own terms. But we figured her out, too. She has sensory integration disorder. Her nerves are so sensitive that sometimes our touch is a shock to her. When she woke during the night, she needed to be changed and to know that we were there. Sometimes, if she initiated it, she would nurse, but the simple comfort of our presence was usually enough. She could dream again.

But those memories were at least five years old when the twins were born and I was filled with fear. What if they didn't sleep well? What if I was up all night every night, first with one and then with the other? I harbored no sentimentality about getting these little guys to sleep. I was militant. I'd feed them once during the night and only after three a.m. After that, they were on their own.

And it worked.

Until they started teething.

On a typical night, the boys will fall asleep between 7 and 8 p.m. and then wake around 5:30 a.m. I'll feed them each a bottle and leave them in their cribs to play. Sometimes, they will go back to sleep until 7. Other times, they'll get up with my husband about 6 a.m. But they've always been good natured about it.

Teething has changed everything.

They had been so good about going back to sleep on their own that I had never bother to figure them out. So when Jonathan woke at 10 the other night and cried and cried and cried, despite a bottle and a diaper change and medicine and attempts at rocking, my husband and I were at a loss. We were up with him for two hours before he could stand it no longer and he crashed. It happened again a few nights later.

I panicked.

What if this became a habit? Our oldest son has trouble falling asleep, so he keeps us up later than we'd like. He'll lie there for an hour or two pondering important things like whether a spider that lost a leg would grow it back exactly as it was and how strong that leg would be when he first started walking on it. He is very good about staying in bed, but I just can't fall asleep when he's awake. So I wait.

Our daughter has her own issues. She is very intelligent and a perfectionist. With that comes high anxiety and vivid nightmares most every night. So she usually wakes up once, and climbs into our bed until she feels better, comforted by the reality around her. Then we bring her back to bed. Her pediatrician believes she will get better with age and she is improving, but it's going to be a long road.

That is hard enough.

I couldn't bear the thought of being up with the twins as well. On those two nights when Jonathan woke up, I barely got three hours of sleep and what I did get was interrupted. So last night when Matthew woke up shoving his fist in his mouth, I tried a different approach. I didn't even change him. He was wearing a night diaper and had only been in bed for an hour. Instead, I gave him a little Tylenol and started rubbing his back. About ten minutes later, he was asleep.

Jonathan woke an hour after that and I tried the same method.

It worked again.

It was then that I realized how much I'd been missing out on with the twins. I sing to them while they sit in front of me on the living room floor, but I don't sing to them while I rock them in my arms like I did with the other two. I can't. When I try, the other twin crawls up to the chair and tries to pull his way into my lap. Then he cries.

I don't carry them around the house on my hip while I do chores, talking them through each step to help improve their vocabulary. Instead, I let them wander more and explore every nook of the house. I show them flashcards with animals on them and make funny noises. I let them crawl all over me while I lie on the floor.

I don't cuddle them on my lap while I read them book after book after book. I can't do that, either. They are too wild. They grab the books out of my hands even if I give them other books as distractions. So I read to them after meals while they sit in their highchairs.

It got me thinking. It got me thinking that I am not as in tune with them as individuals and worrying that the lack of intimacy will somehow hurt their emotional development. Maybe I should try harder. Maybe I'm being too selfish. Then I caught myself doing it. I razzed Jonathan's belly and kissed him all over his head and neck after I changed him on the changing table. I do that almost every time I change him because he loves it.

I scooped up Matthew and saw that look on his face that said he was about to plant a kiss on my cheek, so I held him close and whispered, "Kisses, kisses, kisses" while he soaked my cheek with his love. Then I swung him around. He loves to be flipped, swung and bounced. Sometimes, I mix the boys up for just a second. Then one of them does something. He moves a certain way. He makes a particular sound. He lunges for one toy instead of another. And I know instantly who it is.

The thing is I am not bonding with one baby. This is different and it doesn't work in such a linear way. I am bonding with two individuals and with the twins as a unit. At the same time, they are bonding with each other. I am not missing out. They are not missing out. It just takes a little longer for each bond to grow and to strengthen because there are so many bonds developing at once. It's just a whole new adventure for all of us.

BE PATIENT

Parents of multiples are often reluctant to talk about the obstacles they face in bonding with their infants. Society expects us to be one with our babies from birth. When we don't feel that bond immediately, sometimes we feel like failures. But the reality is that even parents of singletons don't bond with their babies immediately. Sure, we love them. Who could resist those tiny fingers and toes, those trusting eyes, and that desperate cry? But bonding requires familiarity and familiarity takes time. When parents are trying to bond with more than one baby at once, it takes even longer. Give yourself a break. You love your babies and you know it. The bonding part will happen, and when it does, you'll find it was worth the wait.

TROUBLE TIMES TWO

Ten months

Earlier this morning, I decided to give the boys a bath. I got everything ready and carried Matthew upstairs to the pack-n-play, leaving Jonathan penned in the childproofed living room. At least I thought it was childproofed. In the forty-five seconds or so that it took me to go up the stairs and back down again, Jonathan had used the VCR guard to pull the machine down from the shelf. I found him sitting on the floor in front of the TV with the VCR in his lap, playing with the cords that snaked out of the back.

I was surprised.

That was something Matthew would do.

In the past few weeks, their curiosity has equalized. Matthew had always been the lone troublemaker. He flips on the changing table, desperate to see what might be behind him. He races to the bathroom every time we open the door, hoping to get his hands on the toilet paper. He lunges for the opening when we step through the kitchen gate, determined to slip through before we notice. Through all that, Jonathan would sit and watch.

No more.

Now, it's a competition.

Jonathan can flip with every bit as much muscle as Matthew on that changing table. They have learned that they can both squeeze through the bathroom door together. Whoever makes it through the kitchen gate first usually turns quickly around and slams the gate shut on the other. My self-assurances that the wilder twin's behaviors would forever be balanced with an milder brother are dashed. We're in trouble.

KEEPING TWINS SAFE

It's hard enough to childproof a home for one baby, but two? Two babies require a whole new level of vigilance. Here are few tips derived from my own experience in trying to keep my two guys out of harm's way:

Create a safe zone. For our boys, we gated off the entire living room area and placed a safety guard over the television and

VCR. This was in the days of huge, bulky TVs. We secured the entertainment center to the wall and ensured that they could not pull the TV down. We had to climb over or pass through gates to access any other room in the house but it was worth it. I could let my guard down a bit when they played in this zone because I knew it was free of the usual dangers.

Locks, locks and more locks. Place child locks on toilet seat covers, refrigerator doors, cabinets and drawers. You might curse them at first, but the motions required to release the locks will soon become second nature. We also placed safety guards over our oven controls.

Secure all dressers and bookshelves to walls. Many parents put this off until their babies are walking, but it might be too late by then. Babies learn to walk by pulling themselves up with anything their little hands can find. That stage begins sooner than you might think.

Cover all electrical outlets and surge protectors. Child safety products are available at most home improvement and department stores.

Learn to tune out distractions. If someone comes to the door or the phone rings, ignore it unless you are sure you can answer it without putting either baby in danger. The caller will leave a message or call back. The person at the door will just have to wait.

Bathe your twins separately in this first year and never leave either child alone in the tub for even a second. Gather everything you need before bath time and have it on hand. Leave a checklist in the bathroom if it helps.

Take your own needs into consideration. In those first days, I so often found myself physically occupied but mentally bored. Don't get me wrong, I enjoyed my twins—their expressions, their giggles, the sweet smell of their skin—but sometimes I needed a mental break. So I stashed novels everywhere. I had one on each of our three floors, usually beside the chair I nursed in. How does this relate to safety? If you are bored, you are more likely to get up and leave the babies for a moment to fetch your iPod, check your email or browse through Facebook. You wouldn't leave your babies in a room with no entertainment. Don't deprive yourself either.

TEAMWORK

Ten months

Matthew and Jonathan have learned to work as a team.

Just two days ago, at nearly eleven months old, they simultaneously grabbed the top of the gate that divides the living room from the foyer, keeping them safe from all the dangers that lurk beyond. They pulled themselves up and started shaking it with huge grins on their faces.

I glanced.

I grinned in returned.

I walked away.

Moments later, I heard a crash.

They had torn the gate down.

I am so naive.

THE EXPERTS

Ten months

I received a newsletter the other day via email from a popular parenting website. The weekly newsletters are generated according to the babies' ages. They are intended to enlighten parents about developmental milestones while also offering tips for coping, feeding, sleeping -you name it. This particular issue focused on interaction with peers.

"For the most part," the experts write, "babies this age parallel play, staying happily engrossed in their own activities alongside one another, but without really interacting. This is normal — focusing on their own abilities and needs is how they develop. Over time, though, you'll notice your baby stealing glances at fellow babies, and she may crawl over to try to use the same toy."

Clearly, they have not studied twins.

Soon after I read this, I watched Matthew chase Jonathan on hands and knees from the living room, through the gate and into the kitchen. Once they reached the tile floor, Jonathan sat, turned in Matthew's direction and started laughing. Matthew stopped, looked at his brother and laughed in return. And they were not just giggling. These were deep, honest, belly laughs.

A moment later, they were at it again, heading toward the dining room at full speed. This chase-sit-laugh-and-repeat game continued for about ten minutes. It ended when they reached the bookshelf. Unfortunately, for them, my husband and I had removed the books that they had so enjoyed taking off the shelves and shredding.

As I have mentioned previously, Matthew and Jonathan have interacted with growls, grunts and other noises since they were four months old. Now, each nap or bedtime begins with the two of them standing up, hanging onto their crib rails and shaking them with all their might while exchanging laughter.

Toys have been a problem since the boys began to scoot at about six months. The rattle, ball or block in the other baby's hand is always much more fun. Tug-of-wars erupt about every ten or fifteen minutes. Several of the most controversial toys have gotten time-outs atop the entertainment center.

And let's not forget empathy.

Matthew has developed a habit of pushing food out between what few teeth he has and letting it slide out of his mouth. He seems to like the sensation of applesauce flooding his chin and neck. I decided I had to nip this habit. So, the other day, I issued a scolding "no" as soon as I saw the food beginning to emerge.

Matthew seemed startled. Then his eyes scrunched, his lips quivered and the tears began. Jonathan looked over at his brother. They locked eyes for an instant and suddenly the same sorrowful expression washed over him. Within seconds, both boys were sobbing uncontrollably in their highchairs.

I find it hard to believe their level of interaction is unique. I'm guessing that it is common for twins, whether identical or fraternal, to begin interacting at earlier ages. It requires different parenting strategies than those recommended by the experts. For instance, I probably would have kept scolding Matthew if he were a singleton until the stream from his mouth dried up. But he won. I'm tough enough to handle one set of quivering lips, but not two.

Dribble away.

COOPERATIVE PLAY

We don't need scientists to confirm that identical twins are quicker to develop cooperative play skills than their singleton peers. Simply peruse YouTube with the search terms "identical twins" and "babies" and "play" and you'll find video after video of infant and toddler twins entertaining each other.

MIXED-UP MOM

Ten months

Mischievous giggles drew me into the nursery this afternoon. Both boys should have been fast asleep. I had put them down for naps more than half an hour before and they were exhausted. But there, in Jonathan's crib, stood the most irresistible little bundle of a guy, smiling, drooling and shaking his crib with vigor. I lifted him out and pulled him close to me, letting him rest his cheek against mine. It was something Matthew would normally do. Jonathan is more likely to snuggle into my neck. But things always change with these guys. They pick mannerisms and habits up from each other.

We stayed that way for a few moments and then moved into the living room. For the next twenty minutes, I cuddled him and played with him on the floor. I held him up to the mirror and said, "There's Jonny!" I played, "How big is Jonny? Sooooo big!" I whispered, "Mommy loves you, Jonny," over and over again in his ear.

Then came a short cry from the nursery.

The baby I lifted from Matthew's crib snuggled into my neck. I pulled him away and looked at the vein across his nose. Nausea washed through my stomach. I had mixed them up before. For a moment. Maybe two. But never for this long. I'm sure that in a few days, maybe even in a few hours, I'll find the humor in this. But, right now, it's lost to me.

RELAX

It has been a few years now and I have found the humor in this incident. Relax. These things happen. Keep in mind your twins are babies and they will have no memory of incidents like this. By the time they are old enough to remember, they will have differentiated enough in personality that mix-ups are unlikely. And if it happens? If you do mix them up? They will probably laugh right along with you.

RANTERS AND RAVERS
Eleven months

I was perusing an online bulletin board yesterday for moms of multiples when I came across a thread of rants about people who stop moms and comment on their twins in malls, in grocery stores, in Target and in Wal-Mart. One woman was furious with people who praise her older daughter for being such a good helper. "Come on people. She's only three," she wrote. Another could not believe anyone would ask whether her babies were, indeed, twins. A third was insulted by people who ask her how she handles it all.

People can be so rude, can't they?

No, no, no. I'm not talking about the folks who make the comments. I am referring to those twin moms. Sure it can be tough sometimes. I've had my share of incidents. One man insisted my twins were not identical. He just wouldn't give up. So I did. A clerk in a department store once blocked my way. She just stood there ogling the boys for several minutes. When I tried to get around her, she stepped in my path again. She persisted until another clerk pulled her away. A neighbor's nine-year-old son once grabbed one baby by the face and screamed in another baby's ear (We stay away from them now.).

But that's three incidents in eleven months. And they were real. It was not a matter of perception. They were incidents I had a right to complain about. What I am learning, however, is that a minority of moms of multiples simply like the attention they get when they complain. They enjoy perceiving themselves as "victims" of such comments and they enjoy being part of an exclusive club in which innocent remarks made by non-members somehow raise their status. It's a club in which non-members (parents of singletons and non-parents) are perceived as naïve, brazen and intentionally cruel.

Before I had twins, I was not versed in twin etiquette. I had never referred to any twins as "double trouble" and I can't imagine that I ever would. But the people who have said it to me have done so with humor, as an ice-breaker of sorts. It's been a precursor to kinder, more thoughtful remarks. I have not been insulted, nor would have considered that acknowledging the difficulties of juggling twins or complimenting a three-year-old sibling would be rude, either. I am more likely to appreciate the sympathy and the attention given to my older children.

Many of the comments on that thread were funny and light-hearted. Moms and dads shared humorous or politely corrective come-backs that few of us ever think of in the heat of the moments. But there were those few twin moms who just seemed to get a high off of the opportunity to be haughty in return. Their babies are their power trips.

It's a shame.

Some folks are a little overwhelmed when they see twins, especially identical twins it seems. They want to say something. Anything. And they don't hire speech writers. It just comes out. Sometimes, it comes out beautifully. Other times, the result is awkward. Can't we cut them a little slack?

My boys are a blessing. They are not double trouble, I don't really need sympathy and sometimes I get exasperated when errands take me three times longer than they should because so many people stop to greet the boys. But when I do feel myself becoming exasperated, I think of the smiles and I remember how easily the twins can brighten a day, simply by their existence. How selfish that would be of me to deny someone that moment.

There was one mom on that thread who saw the light. She was shopping with four of her children, including her twins. A woman asked whether they were all hers. She felt that rage, the urge to be rude, rising inside her, but she decided to fight it this time. She smiled and said that yes, they were.

"I almost cried right there," she wrote. "She had two kids like five or so years apart and she wished they were closer in age. We had a great conversation for the few seconds my wildness would allow."

Thank goodness she let her wild side rule.

RUNNING ERRANDS EFFICIENTLY

It's hard enough to run errands with one baby, but twins tend to be show-stoppers. Everybody wants a peek and that can seriously hamper your efforts to get things done. It is possible though to yield to that curiosity and still tick everything off your list with your sanity intact. Here are few tips for running errands more efficiently:

Build in plenty of extra time. If you simply accept that you will spend a certain amount of time dealing with oglers, you will be less irritated by the distractions. Plan your escapes ahead. Come up with polite lines for ending conversations like, "I'd better get moving before they get hungry," and then move. Start pushing the stroller again as an indication that time is up. If you are in a big hurry, don't stop. Smile apologetically and keep going.

Do not dress your twins alike. That is asking for attention.

Be prepared. Make sure you are equipped for any kind of baby-emergency so your trip won't be cut short. Fill your diaper bag with food, drinks, diapers, wipes, change of clothes, toys.

Prioritize. Tackle the most urgent errands first.

Consolidate your errands so you make as few trips in and out of stores as possible. This might require some compromises. For instance, you might have gone to a favorite bakery for bagels before you had your twins. Post-twins, buy your bagels from the grocery store's bakery while you do the rest of your food shopping. Get stamps at the grocery store while you're there and save a trip to the post office.

If you have a spouse or partner, run some errands when he or she is home and leave the twins behind. I found it relaxing to grocery shop at ten at night when my husband wasn't traveling. No lines to fight and no babies to entertain.

Hire a sitter. Yes, sitters are expensive, but they can save you money as well. You might find you are a wiser and more selective shopper without the distraction of two little ones. The savings can outweigh the cost of the sitter.

SURVIVING CHRISTMAS
Eleven months

We were proud of ourselves.

We had pulled out a pack-n-play Christmas Eve and set it up near the television. We had a Wiggles DVD ready to go. We figured the boys could tear through their stockings in the pack-n-play the next morning. When the novelty wore off, they could watch Greg, Murray, Jeff and Anthony do "The Flap." Hopefully, that would keep them entertained and keep everyone else's gifts intact until breakfast. After breakfast, we could try naps.

I never thought it could be simpler than that.

Jonathan and Matthew awoke around six a.m. to a tree surrounded by gifts for them, their grandparents, their older brother, their sister, my husband and me. It was a sea of clashing colors, glitter and patterns. It was the ultimate temptation. It was irresistible even for me.

The older kids were not up yet, so we decided to put the babies down for a bit to see how they reacted. They were off as soon as they touched the floor. On hands and knees, they flew past the gifts, past the tree and over to the opening in the gate that divides the living room from the kitchen.

They left it all behind for the dog door, the air vents and chairs that can be slid back and forth across the tile and the hardwood. And there they stayed most of the morning, happy just to be free.

WHAT TO GIVE?

At this age, keep in mind your twins have no idea what gifts are, that they are supposed to receive any, or whether they received more or less than anyone else. This is your one opportunity to keep it simple with no repercussions. Give them a few things you believe will entertain them or help in their development, but don't stress. Enjoy!

TOWARD WALKING
Eleven months

I lie on the floor and within a few seconds, Matthew is there. He places both hands on my tummy and gets into a squat position. Then he sticks his butt up in the air and his hands come off my body. Suddenly, he is standing above me, all thirty-one inches of him. His hands are in the air at first, but slowly, as he grows confident in his balance, they drop to his sides. He grins. I applaud. He falls onto his bottom and laughs.

Jonathan would never do that.

For two little boys who look alike, eat alike and laugh alike, their approaches to walking couldn't be more different. While Matthew is determined to stand unassisted, Jonathan simply giggles and buckles his knees when I try to encourage him to lock his legs with no other support. But he buckles them slowly, using his quad strength to lower himself gently to the floor. Jonathan prefers to practice his balance while in motion. He focuses on bridging the gaps between the coffee table and the recliner and the coffee table and the sofa. Like our older children, he will likely bridge that gap hands-free one day and the era of walking will begin. Matthew is taking the harder path, but it doesn't matter. Whoever succeeds first will lead the other.

That's what they do, these brothers.

WHEN TO WORRY

Identical twins should meet their milestones around the same time, but not necessarily at precisely the same time. If one child is walking and the other is not, give him time. The other twin will likely come around within a few days. But trust your instincts as well. If that lag time becomes significant, contact your pediatrician and ask for a referral for evaluation.

THE BIRTHDAY LOOMS

Eleven months

In just ten days, the boys will be one year old. With that pending milestone comes a new slew of questions from friends, family, casual acquaintances and even strangers.

How are we going to celebrate?

My husband and I hadn't given it much thought. Cake, ice cream and a few gifts with just the six of us: that was the plan. The more children you have, the more you realize that first birthday parties are for the parents and the siblings, not the child who is approaching toddlerhood. After all, the birthday boys won't know what is happening or remember a thing. Still, I was curious. Was there something different we should be doing?

So I started researching online. It so happens the topic is hot on online bulletin boards for moms of infant twins. In the interest of promoting separate identities, many parents out there will be baking separate cakes, singing the birthday song to each child separately and, in one case, even sending out separate invitations. Panic began to set in, but it was short-lived. Separate cakes, I can understand. But separate birthday songs? And forget about separate invitations.

This is the one day of the year we should really celebrate the fact that Matthew and Jonathan are twins. Not just any twins, but identical twins. They share DNA, they shared my uterus and they share a birthday. They have a bond that no parents can give siblings no matter how badly they might want to. Their status as twins, especially as identical twins, is a gift. It is a blessing, and we still wonder why we were so fortunate.

We are too tired for a big celebration, so it will be just the six of us. It has been a wonderful, but exhausting, year and I am sure the celebrations will grow as they age. Regardless, there are three things I know will not change: Matthew and Jonathan will share a birthday cake (at least until they are old enough to ask for their own), they will share the birthday song and their names will always appear on one invitation. We will do this because who they are together is vital to their identities as individuals.

YOU MADE IT!

Your twins are the center of attention on this first anniversary of their birth, but don't forget to acknowledge the other super star on this date: You! You did it! You survived what will probably be the most demanding period of your twins' lives. Other stages will present their own challenges, but sleep deprivation and lack of experience handling two infants at a time make infancy especially difficult. Give yourself a hug! You deserve it.

PART 2

On the Move

(Ages 1 to 3 years)

The toddler years can be the most challenging for any parent. This is the stage of newfound mobility, speech and independence. Our twins need our constant attention and guidance as they test the limits of their worlds. They will run off in different directions at the same time, attract double the attention when they melt down in grocery stores and take their frustrations out on each other when things don't go their way. Somedays, you will want to tear your hair out. But you won't because right at that moment, just when you think you are going to lose it, they will do something, discover something or say something that will make you smile inside and out. These years can be as rewarding as they are challenging. Take care of yourself, accept help when it is offered and, most importantly, nurture your sense of humor. Laughter is the most valuable tool you have.

TODAY THEY ARE ONE

One year

When I first discovered I was carrying twins nearly twenty-one weeks into my pregnancy, I was relieved to learn my doctor was confident they were fraternal. I feared identical twins. I feared mixing them up. I feared others mixing them up. I feared that I would fail to nurture their individual personalities. Today, on the anniversary of their births, I have to laugh at myself.

Though I have mixed them up on occasion, I did so simply because I wasn't paying attention. Other people mix them up all the time, but they usually ask for clarification, which I happily provide. As for their personalities, they are, to me, nothing alike.

At their one-year, well-child check today, both babies were thirty-two inches tall. Their heads measured the same and Jonathan weighed a bit more than Matthew at twenty-six pounds (Matthew weighed more than Jonathan last time).

Yet they have their physical differences. Matthew has a narrow vein across the bridge of his nose while Jonathan's is thick. Jonathan has fuller cheeks than his twin. Today, Jonathan has two scratches on his face, both from Matthew's attempts to play ball with his head. Their personality differences are less obvious to those who do not know them well, but clear to my husband, their older siblings and me.

Jonathan seeks independence when it comes to feeding. He steals the spoon from our hands, he has insisted on feeding himself since about eight months old and he learned to hold a sippy cup almost the day we gave it to him. Matthew is content to be fed. He eats finger foods, but he enjoys slurping banana pudding off a spoon that magically appears near his mouth. He just recently started holding his own sippy cup. He has found that it is much more fun, however, to throw the cup on the hardwood floor.

Matthew does not sit still. He pursues his brother relentlessly, using Jonathan's head and body to pull himself to a standing position. He likes to be cuddled, but only for a moment because he might miss something. He is the worst of the two when it comes to diaper changes. His back arches and his body contorts the instant we lay him down. He is strong. Changing him is more than a battle; it is a whole war over and over again.

Jonathan falls happily into our arms and likes to stay there for a while. He gets excited when his twin brother comes crawling toward him with that particular I'm-going-to-get-you laugh, naive to the punishment that is about to come. We can sometimes (rarely, but sometimes) distract Jonathan during a diaper change.

So on this day - their first birthday - I get a chuckle out of that huge, pregnant woman who feared having two babies who look alike. I am no expert in raising twins and certainly no expert in raising identical twins, but this is what having identical twins has come to mean for me so far: It means that when I am having a bad day and I just need to know people are generally good and that there are a lot of caring and loving people out there, I can dress the boys alike and take them to the mall. I rarely dress them alike, but when I do, they are showered with attention, good attention. Attention that helps me remember how blessed I am with all four of our children and how little all the nasty details of life really mean.

KEEPING IT POSITIVE

Raising twins is tough. No doubt about it. But it is even harder when you are immersed in self-pity or swimming in negativity. I have often been asked how I maintained such a positive attitude when the twins were so young. Our older children were in grade school when Matthew and Jonathan were born, my husband traveled frequently and we had no family nearby to help. It was overwhelming at times. But this is how I did it:

Whenever those negative feelings threatened to settle in, I thought of a friend who lost her baby at thirty-eight weeks. Her pregnancy had been blissfully routine. The nursery was ready and Christmas was just a few weeks away. She and her husband looked forward to celebrating a new year with their two older girls and their new addition.

We had just returned home from visiting them when the phone rang. It was her husband and he was in tears. The baby had turned in utero and the umbilical cord had wrapped around her neck. She was stillborn. It was no one's fault and it could not have been predicted or prevented. I was miles away when they lost their baby, but I was devastated for them. I couldn't even begin to imagine their pain. I felt so helpless.

Then I became pregnant with twins.

In comparison, the trials of raising twins seemed trivial. I had two healthy, thriving babies and two older children who would all grow up someday and need me less intensely. I was fortunate to be needed at all and I have tried to savor every second of it. I have had my moments. Haven't we all? But that's what they were—moments. I did not let them define me and I did not let them define my relationship with my children.

When you are tempted to give in to negativity, try to put the situation into perspective and determine what is really getting you down. Is there one thing you can do to make it better? Focus on the solutions instead of traveling down that negative road. Little things helped me, like singing when twins were crying or keeping one novel on each level of the house, so I could feel like a grown-up amid the physical demands of child care. Antics that might have inspired anger made people laugh on Facebook, and that made me laugh, too. My husband was (and still is) my rock. He convinced me to write the blog, which pulled me back into freelancing and writing fiction. He helped me retain my sense of self.

If that doesn't work, do not be ashamed to seek professional help. Sometimes, childbirth can shift the chemistry in your brain. You might need a little more of the chemicals your brain already produces to get that balance back. It's not a big deal, especially if it helps you be a better parent. A happy mom is a good mom. Remember that.

IMMUNITY

One year

The differences between the boys are becoming more apparent. Unfortunately, it doesn't bode well for Matthew. Both boys caught a stomach virus a few weeks ago. Matthew threw up longer and more often than his brother. At their one-year appointment a week later, Matthew was a pound lighter than Jonathan. Now they both have colds. It started with runny noses nine days ago. Then Matthew developed a chesty, mucus-laden cough. I took him to the doctor's when I noticed he would sometimes stop playing and scream for a minute.

The doctor checked both boys. Jonathan is fine. Still no cough. Still just a runny nose. Matthew has an ear infection and this time, he was a one pound, 10 ounces lighter than his brother. He still has the nasty cough, but his chest is clear. The antibiotics should kick in tomorrow.

Though Matthew apparently has a lower resistance to illness than Jonathan, he proved last night that he is stronger in other ways: he took his first independent steps. So Matthew will get better soon, probably just a few days after his brother. And Jonathan will be walking soon, probably just a few days after his brother.

IMMUNITY IS NOT INHERITED

Nine years have passed since I wrote that blog post and, in that time, Jonathan and Matthew have contracted and fought countless bacterial and viral infections. Sometimes, Matthew recovered faster. Other times, Jonathan was the stronger of the two. But I cannot recall a time when one was sick and the other was not. I assumed the pattern would remain unchanged as long as they continued to shares sips of drinks or bites of food.

Not so, according a 2015 study conducted at Stanford University.

The study shows that only about 25 percent of our immunity is inherited. The rest develops over time with exposure to various microbes, toxins and vaccinations, and through differences in diet and dental hygiene. Our bodies are continually adapting to these encounters and the adaptations overshadow our inherited responses, according to the study. So it makes sense that when identical twins are young and are sharing the same physical environment, their immune reactions will be similar. But as they become adults, their immune systems will differentiate. A shared drink will no longer guarantee a shared virus.

ASSUMPTIONS AND BLESSINGS
One year, one month

One of the first lessons I learned as a journalist was never to make assumptions. Don't assume all siblings share the same last name. Don't assume that beer bottles in a car mean the driver was drinking. Don't assume that you can even begin to comprehend someone else's pain. It is a lesson I have tried to apply to my personal life as well.

So when a woman I had become casual friends with through my oldest son began to drift away, I assumed nothing. We were not very close. Our older children landed in different classrooms this year and she had taken a part-time job. I tried not to assume that it was personal, but I learned yesterday that it was.

Her daughter and mine are in the same class this year and have become friends. They insisted on a playdate and it finally happened yesterday. I noticed that the mom watched the twins play when she dropped her daughter off and seemed interested in them, even drawn to them. But she kept her distance. Soon after she left, her daughter told me her older brother was a twin, but that his twin had died before birth.

When the woman returned to retrieve her daughter, I apologized for my ignorance and for any insensitivity I might have displayed during my pregnancy and after. I offered my condolences, unsure whether I was doing or saying the right thing. But relief seemed to wash over her. And she talked.

She talked about learning her son had died inside her body at twenty weeks. She talked about the doctors removing the baby and the sac, careful not to touch the surviving baby. She talked about seven long weeks in the hospital on full bed rest and the one-pound, twelve-ounce baby who struggled so hard to survive. She talked about how blessed and grateful they are that the tiny little baby did survive and that he has no problems resulting from his prematurity. She talked about medical miracles and her familiarity with the NICU.

She did not talk about the pain of her loss or the pain that I now recognize on her face as she watches my boys play.

This time, I decided, it was safe to make an assumption: She is strong in a way that I am not sure I could ever be. I meet people like her around every corner, people who have lost children. And every day, I think of them. I think of them when the frustration mounts. When the twins are crying, the older kids won't do their homework, dinner is burning, the laundry is piling up, I have no time to write and I've barely slept for days.

I am reminded that I have four healthy children, a wonderful husband and a stepdaughter who loves us all. I might have frustrations, but I do not carry that sorrow in my heart that she will have forever. I do not have to be so strong. Life is good. I can handle it.

WHAT DO YOU SAY TO PARENTS HAVE LOST A TWIN?

Thankfully, I have never been the subject of this question, but I have encountered many women over the years who have lost a twin. My experience with my friend taught me to look for the signs. But what do you say when you learn of their losses? It's an odd situation. You want to be happy for the birth of the healthy child, but you also need to recognize and appreciate their grief. The question came up once on an online forum I participated in. Here a few suggestions from moms who lost twins themselves:

Just be there. People tend to avoid uncomfortable situations and that can be cruel in a case like this. Stop by to visit, bring a meal or offer your support. Provide a distraction and a sounding board. Be a friend.

Don't avoid the subject, especially if the parents show a desire to talk. Talking about loss is a huge part of the grieving process. You can't take away the pain, but you can help them process it just by being a good listener.

Don't suggest that they distract themselves from the pain by focusing on the living child. It is usually well-intended, but nothing and no one can take the place of the lost child. Let them grieve.

Do something. Some people on the forum were comforted by friends who redesigned their nurseries, removing the extra crib and clothing so they wouldn't have to. Others were appreciative of memorial gifts, like pillows with the lost child's name embroidered on them or jewelry engraved with the child's name. Holiday ornaments memorializing the child were also well-received.

Refer them to the Center for Loss in Multiple Birth (http://www. climb-support.org/). The group brings together people who have suffered the loss of one or more babies during pregnancies with multiples. Sometimes it helps just to know you are not alone.

TO DRESS ALIKE OR NOT TO DRESS ALIKE

One year, two months

I had to laugh when I read the post from a new mother of twins on an online bulletin board. She was frustrated. She had expressed her desire early in her pregnancy to always dress her babies differently, yet her mother-in-law continued to give them gifts of matching outfits. She wondered whether anyone could help her get her point across.

"This is something I have strong feelings about," she wrote. "I do not believe they should be dressed alike. No offense to anybody out there who does it, this is just my opinion."

That was me 14 months earlier. I was determined never to dress our guys alike, especially since they were identical. Coordinating outfits, I could deal with, but I wouldn't dress them in anything that fully matched. I wasn't going to be that person and they were not going to be those kids. Then one day, it happened.

I dove into their dresser to search for an outfit. I had planned to take them on errands and I wanted to make sure they wore the same weight clothing so that each would be as warm as the other. The easiest solution was clothing that matched. Guess what? I did it and nothing happened.

They didn't start answering to each other's names. They didn't eat with each other's hands. They didn't confuse their feet or fingers or their toes with the other's. Matthew still seemed to know he was Matthew and Jonathan still seemed to know he was Jonathan.

It was a miracle.

What really happened is that I learned to relax. I don't stress out about the fact that they rarely go anywhere separately. I don't get worked up when someone mistakenly calls them by the wrong names. I usually dress them differently, but every now and then, if I am in the mood or if I am out of clothing, I dress them alike.

My husband and I give them plenty of space to develop their individuality, but we don't force it on them. Matthew and Jonathan already have personalities that are as different as night and day, so why should we interfere? By the time they are three, or maybe even two, they will develop preferences and they will assert them. One day they will demand different clothing. Another day they will get great pleasure out of dressing alike. The choices will be theirs, not ours.

And we will do our job.

We will listen to my two very different little boys.

IDENTICALLY CLINGY

One year, two months

I knew I was in trouble about a week ago when Matthew stood up in front of me, lifted his watery blue-gray eyes to meet mine and then raised his arms with that sad, lonely, needy look. That look was familiar.

I remembered it from my oldest son when he was about fifteen months old and from my daughter at about the same age, and I knew it was only a matter of days before Jonathan raised his arms with the same pleading, heart-breaking gaze. They seem to hit these emotional milestones together. I was right and now I am exhausted.

They have reached the age of separation anxiety. Not the don't-leave-me-with-someone-else-or-I'll-cry-my-eyes-out-and-make-you-feel-like-a-bad-mom kind. I'll think we'll get away without experiencing too much of that. They have each other and they seem to take comfort in their relationship whenever I leave them.

No. This is worse. With the other kind of separation anxiety, you can be pretty sure that after you've been gone for five minutes, the caretaker will distract them and they'll forget all about you until they see your face again and remember that the show must go on, restarting the tears they had put on hold.

No. This is the I-want-to-be-in-mommy's-arms-twenty-four-hours-a-day-and-don't-you-dare-pick-up-my-brother kind. I get nothing done and neither is ever happy unless I manage to stay out of sight. If they can't see me, they are content. They play well together and are thrilled to be dumping their toys bins, throwing blocks and pushing chairs around the kitchen.

But when they see me, I am surrounded by desperate arms and a moat of tears. If I pick both up at once, they start to wail and cry and push each other away. If I am holding one and the other even comes near, the tears flow from the baby above and the baby below. I can't win.

I either walk around with a baby on one hip, trying to dodge the other for a while until it's time to switch, or I hide out altogether, penning them in the living room and peering around the door way to check on them occasionally. I've asked other twin moms how they've handle this, but the only hopeful answer I get is that they grow older each day and that everything will get better as they age.

I know. I know.

I don't want them to grow up too fast and I am flattered that they need me so much, but can't we just skip a few months here? Turn clocks ahead a little just past the separation anxiety stage? I'm even willing to move right into tantrums. Even the really loud, embarrassing ones. Please?

FREEDOM AT LAST

One year, two months

The weather was beautiful this past weekend, so we took the boys outside for their first opportunity to wander on foot. They are not fully walking yet, so we gave them their push toys and set them free in the cul de sac.

We thought they would at least stay together. After all, they are identical twins, who, because life gets in the way and (honestly) it's easier for me, rarely get to go anywhere without each other. No way.

Neither could care less where the other brother was. They bolted in opposite directions, exploring the pavement, the grass, the sidewalks and our neighbors' garages. Their push toys were their vehicles. They put them in fifth gear and went at full speed.

Yet, both Matthew and Jonathan gripped the handle in that same fiercely-determined way. They both focused on their targets straight ahead, ignoring the teens playing basketball, the two sets of parents out with their preschoolers and their brother and sister, who were running and scootering to keep up with them.

They both preferred lawns to pavement. They both were attracted to the neighbor's seven dogs when they let them out to play (Yes, they have seven. They also have eleven cats). They both turned bright red from the heat of the day and their exertion after about forty minutes, stumbling, crying and struggling to go on when their little legs could take no more.

They both fought to remain outside and guzzled just about equal amounts of water when we finally carried them, kicking and wailing, into the house. They both ate a ton for dinner that evening. It makes me wonder.

When we put them to bed that night and they stood in their cribs facing each other, playing their little game where they grab each other's hands, peel them off the crib rails and laugh when the other falls, were they comparing notes from their outing or did they even have to? Did they already know?

SPOON WARS

One year, three months

There are some things identical twins do that we parents take for granted. Today, for the first time, I really thought about the spoons. It's automatic now. Each time I feed the boys yogurt or cereal or mashed sweet potatoes, I bring three spoons to the table. I can usually get through a few mouthfuls before it happens: one of the boys clenches the rubbed-tipped utensil in his teeth, using every muscle in his little jaws to protect his claim.

As he proudly displays the metal handle that juts from his mouth, he gets a sideways glance from his brother who returns the look with what

I swear is a nod. I reach for a new spoon and lift the food to the mouth of the other twin. Sure enough, his brother clenches in the same manner, claiming a spoon for his own.

Victory is theirs.

Defeated, I pick up spoon number three.

THE "FAT" ONE

One year, three months

It happened again two days ago.

I was taking the boys on a two-mile walk through the neighborhood. The day was a little too warm and the sky was cloudless. A slight breeze took the edge off the heat. Matthew and Jonathan had tummies full of milk, were fresh from a nap and were happy to take in the houses, the trees, the birds and the smell of fresh-cut grass. They felt good. I felt good.

Then, about ten minutes into our excursion, a minivan pulled over. The driver's side window came down and a woman I'd met only twice before stuck her head out. She wanted a glimpse of the twins. I obliged. Within less than a minute, I regretted it.

"So let's see," she said. "He's the fat one."

She pointed at Matthew, who had just dropped a pound below his brother due to the loss of appetite that came with a bout of the roseola virus. I was dumbstruck. I found myself stumbling over my words, trying to explain that, generally, the boys are only a few ounces apart. If anything, Jonathan's cheeks are a bit fuller than Matthew's.

I should have been prepared. This happens all the time and it happened again half a mile down the road. A woman was trying to help her granddaughter differentiate between the boys and, this time, she identified Jonathan as "the fat one."

For some people, our boys are like that puzzle I often see in children's magazines, the one where two pictures look identical and the challenge is to find the differences between them. Certain people seem obsessed with finding differences between our boys and they present their observations as if they might be new to me.

The "fat" observation is their favorite and the one that concerns me the most. Right now, the boys are too young to be bothered. But their comprehension will not always be so limited. I can only hope that people practice more consideration as the boys grow older.

WAKE UP SLEEPYHEAD

One year, three months

Not long ago, when one twin would awaken from a nap before the other, he would relish the time alone with my husband or me. We would cuddle him, read to him, rough-house with him or just carry him around on one hip.

Those days are gone.

Nowadays, we spend that precious alone time trying to distract the wide-eyed twin, who is determined to wake up his brother. They are drawn to each other's cribs like magnets to metal. Eventually, we give in. The awake twin grabs the rails of the sleeping twin's crib, shakes the bars and yells until his brother lifts his head and rubs his eyes. Once his job is done, he toddles away, content knowing that his brother will soon be toddling behind him.

SHARED PAIN OR EMPATHY?

One year, three months

A few months ago, I met an elderly man in the mall who stopped to admire the twins. He is also an identical twin, he said. He shared a story about a day when he was home in Cincinnati and his arm began to ache terribly. He sensed that something was wrong with his twin, who lived five hours away in Cleveland, so he called him several times. No answer. Finally, his twin called him back. He had been in the emergency room with a broken his arm.

"You just wait," the man said with a grin.

I have heard and read many similar stories since the twins were born about identical twins who feel each other's pain, but I was a skeptic. There is no scientific evidence to support it. All the evidence is anecdotal and is, probably, highly exaggerated, I figured. But an incident today made me think again.

I had taken the boys to a Mom's Day Out program that I was considering for the fall. I immediately disliked the place. Several kids played aimlessly in a cramped room while the caretaker sat there like a bump on a log. The director had explained to me that this particular program was simply a babysitting service. But, come on. I would fire any sitter who didn't interact with my kids.

Still, I decided to give it a chance and let my boys play a while. As I was trying to persuade a two-year-old boy that Jonathan's head was not a highway for his dump truck, I heard an ear-piecing scream from Matthew. He was sitting under a table and another boy was crouched behind him. I figured Matthew had tried to stand and had bumped his head. But his reaction was far too strong for that.

Before I could even move, Jonathan looked at Matthew and released an identical scream. And there I stood, between the boys who were crying and screaming so hard that their faces were turning blue (The caretaker, of course, just sat there and did nothing.). Neither boy stopped crying until we left that place.

Later, as I lifted Matthew's shirt to put on his PJs, I found the source of his pain: a perfectly round bite mark from a child who clearly had all of his teeth and knew how to chomp hard enough to break the skin.

Now, mostly likely, Jonathan saw the look on his brother's face and, because they have been together every day since the moment they were conceived, he sensed what Matthew was feeling. Maybe, even at only fifteen months old, Jonathan has already developed empathy. But maybe not.

I am still a skeptic, but I am a skeptic with an open mind, an open mind, that is, toward the concept of the twins feeling each other's pain. My mind is closed to the Mom's Day Out program. When this mom goes out, she'll be bringing her twins.

FRIENDS AT LAST

One year, three months

When Matthew came toddling into the living room the other day carrying Jonathan's stuffed blue puppy (named "Rabbit" because we thought it was a rabbit for the longest time), I prepared for trouble. Rabbit is one of Jonathan's favorite stuffed animals. He sleeps with him every night; he cuddles him when he doesn't feel well; he snuggles with him whenever he goes down for a nap.

But, just as I started to intervene, Matthew shoved Rabbit at his brother, smiled and said "da." Jonathan grinned and hugged Rabbit close to his body. Matthew toddled away and came back with his own stuffed animal, "Beary." The two boys carried their animal friends to the staircase, where they sat side-by-side watching the *Upside Down Show*.

Since then, I have seen similar scenes repeated often.

The boys routinely bring each other sippy cups, toy cars and unused diapers that they have snatched from the changing table. They laugh, they giggle and other strange, new sounds come from their throats. Often, the exchange encourages one twin to join the other twin in an action or a game.

Other signs of this new awareness have surfaced lately as well. Last week, Matthew was sitting in his rocking chair when Jonathan discovered his brother's toes. Jonathan played with Matthew's toes in a game that left them both aching with laughter.

They rarely fall asleep easily now. When I peer between the cracks in their doors long after I have kissed them goodnight, I find them standing in their cribs, grabbing each other's hands over the rails and falling back on their mattresses in giggle fits. Then, they get back up and go at it again.

Jonathan took things a little too far two days ago though when he used Matthew's head as a drum and they still fight over the toy that looks like a telephone, but plays nursery rhyme songs. But when I saw Matthew give Jonathan Rabbit for that first time, it wasn't just his brother he comforted. It was me.

THE REALITY OF TWINESE

One year, four months

"Mmmmwa, mmmmwa."

This is a familiar sound in our house.

We hear it whenever Matthew runs out of Baby Goldfish, raisins, tortellini, bananas or whatever his favorite food of the day might be. He looks up at us with all the confidence in the world and says, "Mmmmwa," his word for "more." And it works. Matthew relishes its results as his request is fulfilled.

Until recently, Jonathan remained quiet. As we praised Matthew and piled more food onto his tray, Jonathan would simply sit and say nothing.

Again and again, I would ask him, "More, Jonny? Do you want more?" And he would just stare at me, eventually crying in frustration until I gave in.

But everything changed just the other day. It was lunch time. Jonathan's tray was empty of green beans, a favorite food of both twins, when I heard that familiar sound coming from his direction.

«Mmmmwa.»

I saw Jonathan's mouth move, but I found myself staring at Matthew. Jonathan said it in exactly the same way and in the same voice. I was stunned. I didn't know what to make of his precise imitation of Matthew's grossly mispronounced word. A few Internet searches later and I had my answer.

This is the beginning of what some people call twinese. I had always believed that twinese was a secret language, a code developed among twins that was independent of our language and that only they could understand. I was wrong. Twinese, scientifically known as idioglossia or cryptophasia, is exactly what I had just witnessed. It occurs when one twin imitates the other in his mispronunciation of words.

When they say the words wrong, they understand each other even if no one else does. If the mispronunciations are not corrected, twins eventually fall into the habit of using the wrong sounds regularly and, what might have seemed cute initially, becomes a problem. They grow older, they start school, and no one else can understand them.

Fortunately, it sounds like we have little to be concerned about. Though twinese is fairly common in the toddler years, studies show that serious cases generally develop when twins are frequently left on their own by parents who are detached from their language development. In most cases, twinese disappears on its own by the preschool years.

CONFUSED AGAIN

One year, four months

For once, I was showered, dressed and wide awake when I took the boys out of their cribs at 6 a.m. yesterday. I grabbed Jonathan mid-bounce and placed him on the changing table. He was calm, which was odd. Jonathan usually contorts his entire body for even the quickest diaper change. I brought him through the kitchen, grabbed his sippy full of milk and set him with his bear on the living room floor.

Next, I grabbed Matthew, who had thrown himself down on the crib mattress, giggling and daring me to pick him up. He was good-natured… until I placed him on the changing pad. His body stiffened instantly. He arched his back and he twisted his hips with a wail. I narrowed my eyes. I held his head between my hands. I focused hard on the vein across his nose. It was thick. I was changing Jonathan.

My husband and I had put Matthew and Jonathan to bed together the night before. We had put them in the wrong cribs with the wrong stuffed animals. The boys are sixteen months old. You'd think we'd know better by now. But still, it happens.

REACHING OUT: BONDS BEYOND THEIR OWN

One year, five months

At eight and a half years old, my oldest son gets not a moment's peace. Riley came down the stairs this morning, bleary-eyed, hungry and sad from the loss of a favorite stuffed animal on a recent trip and he wanted to tell me about it. He didn't get a chance.

His voice was drowned out by the cries and pleas of two younger brothers who stretched out their arms toward him as he lie on the sofa and threw their heads down on its cushions when he failed to pull them up with him. Eventually, Riley gave in.

When I came back in the room with his Ovaltine, he was covered with toddler hands and feet. They climbed over his lap, poked at his face and giggled in his ears. His own tears had dried and so had theirs. Though the bond between identical twins is, indeed, close, these two little guys have found places in their world for their big brother and their older sister.

Huge, special places.

Riley is their rough-houser and cuddler. He chases them round and round the furniture; he roars in their faces; he sneaks them out of their cribs when they are crying and holds them. During the school year, he cannot leave the house until he has had his "fix," he says.

Kiersten took a while to warm up. Drool, wet diapers and (ew!) poopy diapers were a big turn off to her at first. She wanted so badly to hold them when they were babies and she tried, but she just couldn't handle it. But, as they have grown, so has she.

She will be seven at the end of the summer and she has followed the example of her older brother. Though she can still smell a dirty diaper from a mile away, she enjoys teaching them how to play songs on their toy piano, how to build a tower with blocks and how to pronounce the few words they know.

She reads to them, begs to hold them on her lap and even helps put on a fresh diaper now and then. If they get injured, she often cries more than they do. They sometimes call her "mama." They adore her. They adore them both.

I used to worry that the older kids would be jealous of the bond between the boys and that the boys would create their own world, sealing out their older siblings. But there was no need for concern. They have invited them in and Riley and Kiersten have accepted.

WATCH THE HIPS

One year, five months

I was waiting for my daughter at dance camp last week when I ran into a mom who has a son about the same age as the twins. She was leaning over a box of used tap shoes, looking for a pair that would fit her daughter. Her toddler was standing beside her, chewing on a pacifier and clinging to her leg. She asked where the twins were.

"I left them with a sitter," I said. "I can't bring them in here. They'll scream if I leave them in the stroller and they'll run into two different studios if I let them out."

She looked down at her son.

"Not him," she laughed.

That's when it hit me. That's the difference between my twins and so many of their singleton peers. Many toddlers find the world to be a frightening place. They might venture a few feet away from mom or dad in unfamiliar territory, many more than a few if they are certain their parents will chase after them. But, for the most part, they have a necessary sense of wariness about their surroundings. They either wander closely or, like her son, they cling.

Not my twins.

Jonathan and Matthew are full of confidence and lacking in fear no matter where we drop them. They have a routine. They rarely bust into cabinets, yank cloths off tables or topple lamps immediately. They are team and, like any good team, they have a strategy.

First, they explore the entire perimeter, traveling in opposite directions, sometimes faking right or left, but ultimately waiting for the just right moment to put their game plan into action. They wait until the defense is at ease with their movements, until their opponents mistake their intensity for dullness, for a love of repetition.

They simply wait.

Circling, circling, circling.

Until finally their guardians let their guard down.

The break from their circular pattern is sudden and well-executed. They dash in opposite directions, their eyes focused on their targets, energized to tackle any and all obstacles in their way. They are fierce in their purpose and determined to win whether the trophy is an open garbage can, a glass of water perched on the edge of a counter or an adventure in a forbidden room in a house.

We know the way they operate.

We have reviewed the tapes.

So, as we prepare for a trip to Minneapolis this week, where they will meet many of their aunts, uncles and cousins, and see their grandma and grandpa for the first time since they were babies, I have this to say to the reunion attendees: Beware.

Don't be distracted their sweet smiles, their infectious giggles or their blond curls. As my high school soccer coach used the say, if you want to play good defense, watch the hips. It's all in the hips.

BUDDING ARTISTS

One year, six months

Once a month, I tape sheets of white paper to the trays of the boys' high-chairs, slide Matthew and Jonathan into their seats and hand them crayons. I take my own crayons and demonstrate, drawing squares, smiley faces and hearts. Then I watch as they chomp on the crayons and shred the paper.

Today, I prepared for the same scenario, but today was different. Today, they colored.

The pictures are not all that interesting. They are a compilation of scribbles. But what is interesting is this: Jonathan and Matthew did not watch each other or follow one or another's lead. They did not even wait for my demonstration.

On this very same day in this very same moment, they each independently picked up their crayons and put the waxy sticks of color to the paper. They simultaneously achieved the appropriate mix of fine-motor-skill development, curiosity and desire that enabled them to produce scribbles. And when they were done?

They ate the crayons.

LITTLE STRIPPERS

One year, six months

The boys taught each other a few new tricks today. First Jonathan pulled off his shorts. Matthew watched with enthusiasm, stepping out of his own shorts moments later. Cute, I thought, as they ran around the house in their diapers.

I returned to my sink full of dishes.

It was not so cute about five minutes later when Matthew came running into the kitchen fully naked, and proudly handed me his diaper. I peered into the living room, where Jonathan had just managed to peel his diaper off and was holding it up like a trophy.

Grrr.

About an hour ago, I zipped them into sleep sacs--taking comfort in the knowledge that they cannot get their hands inside to strip off their pants and diapers--and I prayed that by tomorrow they will forget. But they won't.

They never forget.

SPEAK! PLEASE?

One year, six months

I'll admit it.

I've been getting a bit paranoid about the twins and their language skills as their eighteen-month appointment approaches (It is scheduled for Monday, about three weeks late.). They seem to understand most everything: They run to their highchairs when I ask whether they want to eat; they bring us their shoes or go to the door when we suggest going outside; they can make a wide variety of animal noises on command.

But they don't really speak.

They have a few clear words. (Well, I can't really think of any that are clear right now, but they do talk a lot.) They practice inflection frequently, usually imitating the true inflection of conversation. They rely heavily on nonverbal expressions, like when they shove books at us, put shoes on our feet or tug on our shirts if we dare try to read the paper, eat some breakfast or even just rest our heads on the table.

Yet when I listen to other toddlers communicate, it just isn't the same.

Despite our best efforts, Jonathan and Matthew are sinking quickly into the language of twinese with such sounds as "nah" for "done" (Where the heck did that come from?) or "seh" for "sit" or "da" for almost anything they want the other twin to see. So, of course, my paranoia led me to Google.

And this is what I found.

According to this recent study, the boys might be behind in language speaking ability, but they are probably right on track as far as overall language development. As twins, they simply tend to use nonverbal skills more often than words.

In fact, they might have an advantage over singletons and twins who do not create their own languages. According to the authors, twin language (or twinese or idioglossia or cryptophasia) enhances language development in a way that is similar to the language enhancement experienced by bilingual children.

Now this study might be flawed. It is based on a small sampling: the children of twenty-six mothers of twins and singletons. It goes against the findings of studies I'd found previously. But, who cares?

Before I googled this study, I was worried that my boys might be behind in their communications skills. These folks say Jonathan and Matthew might, instead, be above average. Their study is good enough for me.

EIGHTEEN MONTHS TALL

One year, six months

They are tall. Boy, are they tall. Three feet tall. That puts Matthew and Jonathan far above the ninety-fifth percentile compared to their male peers, just like our two older kids. We grow them big.

Matthew is the more svelte of the two at twenty-eight pounds, seven ounces, according to the doctor's scale. Jonathan weighed in at twenty-nine pounds, three ounces, during their appointment Monday. Both ranked at the 75th percentile for weight, which makes them long and lean despite their chubby cheeks. Their heads remain in the ninetieth percentile.

Lots of brains, maybe?

The doctor expressed some concern about the development of twinese (or idioglossia or cryptophasia). She said to contact her in three months if they still say no words clearly. The next day, of course, Matthew and Jonathan alternately walked up to our van, patted the side door and said "car" perfectly. Later in the day, they became obsessed with doors, again pronouncing the word clearly.

Earlier this afternoon, they spent fifteen minutes walking from door to door, patting each one and saying "door?" They refused to move on until I said, "Yes, door," with a nod of approval. I had to follow them from room to room or they stomped their feet and cried.

I had planned to drink my coffee.

It got cold.

I didn't mind.

DIFFERENT TOGETHER

One year, six months

People have all kinds of unsolicited advice for parents of identical twins.

Among the most prevalent is that we must do everything possible to encourage separate identities. Dress them differently, buy them their own clothes, separate them in school, take them on separate outings, give them their own bedrooms, never call them "the boys," cut their hair differently, register them for different activities—I could go on and on.

Now, I rarely dress the boys alike, but it's not because I'm pushing some theory on individuality. It's because I'm too lazy. If I dress them differently, I can memorize their clothing in the morning. Then I know who I'm talking to without having to look at the veins on their noses or observe their behaviors for clues.

So that's about all we've done to encourage their individuality.

With two older kids and my husband traveling frequently, we lack the time and the energy to take them on separate outings. I also refuse to dictate their activities as they get older. If they both want to play soccer, then they should both be allowed to play soccer. And recent studies show that identical twins fair better socially and academically in school when placed in the same classrooms. So, if we feel it is in their best interests, we will fight tooth and nail to keep them together.

Yet, individuality happens anyway. Identical twins don't necessarily need a facilitator.

Just the other day, Jonathan started screaming whenever we tried to put him in the newer of the two highchairs. He gladly slides into the older highchair, which he has claimed as his own even though we have always randomly seated them for meals.

Matthew refuses to eat grapes or blueberries even as Jonathan devours them. Sometimes it seems that he refuses them because Jonathan devours them. He watches his brother eat them and then fervently shakes his head "no" when we offer some to him.

Jonathan has even learned to say Matthew's name (Sort of. He says "Maaaahhh!") He looks or points at his brother as he identifies him and then giggles (cackles, really). If asked his own name, he just gets a shy look on his face. "Jon" is hard to say. He doesn't dare try. But he knows that he is not "Maaahhhhh!"

Both boys answer only to their own names.

A sense of self is a product of discovery and discovery occurs when children have choices. Forcing individuality upon identical twins --making them pursue separate activities, separating them in school for no reason other than the notion that separate is better, denying them the chance to decide their own sleeping arrangements as they get older -- is no more admirable than forcing them to be alike.

Like the rest of us, Matthew and Jonathan might never fully understand who they are, but they already know who they are not. Matthew knows he is not Jonathan. Jonathan knows he is not Matthew. To me, that's a successful start.

SNAKES

One year, seven months

Jonathan chewed a long, skinny apple slice down to the peel today. Then he walked around the house, shaking the stringy remnants in the air and saying, "hssssss." A few hours later, I found Matthew slithering along the hardwood in the dining room, dragging himself by his hands. "Hsssss," he said over and over again.

Either they have simultaneously become interested in snakes or they are trying to tell me we have snakes in the house.

Yikes!

LANGUAGE EXPLOSION

One year, seven months

It started about two weeks ago with the light switches. Jonathan suddenly discovered that lights can be turned on and off. He wanted me to flick the switch. I refused. Not until he said, "on." His response was "Ah. Ah."

Good enough.

I flicked the switch to the dining room chandelier, not realizing I was flicking a switch inside his head at the same time. Over the next few days, Jonathan was obsessed with light switches. He took great joy in saying, "Ah. Ah," and in seeing the result.

Soon Matthew joined in and every light in the house had to be on constantly, even during the brightest part of the day. Eventually, we pulled out a couple of stools, placed them under light switches and gave them the power to do it themselves. With that urge satisfied, they began to testing me to see whether words could get them other things.

Matthew pointed to the box of Mini Nilla Wafers on the counter and said, "cookie." After Jonathan got a time-out for standing on a chair to reach the apples, he stood below the basket, pointed and said, "ahhh-pp."

Both boys grinned widely when they realized that saying, "no," was even more fun than simply shaking their heads. They run to the gate blocking the stairs to the second floor at least once a day and say, "bath," with exciting clarity.

Just a month ago, we were talking to the pediatrician about speech therapy if the boys didn't start saying a few clear words soon. Now I have trouble reading books to them because they interrupt constantly, making animal sounds or pointing to objects and attempting to verbalize their names.

The best part? I finally get to hear their voices. Their real voices.

The voices of my identical twins boys.

WRESTLE-CUDDLE FEST

One year, seven months

It was about seven a.m. and the boys had been up for an hour. I was putting shoes away in their room when Jonathan came in, begging to climb into Matthew's crib. As soon as Matthew heard the "squeak-squeak" of his brother's bouncing, he came running and reached up, signaling that he wanted to join his brother.

And so the wrestle-cuddle fest began.

This has become their new ritual, usually after nap time. They meet in Matthew's crib and throw themselves down on the mattress. They cuddle, they wrestle, they laugh and, if I'm not watching them carefully, they sometimes lie on each other's heads. They also kick each other in the face and step on each other's tummies. All in fun, of course.

But today, there was a new development. Today, for the first time, Matthew kissed Jonathan. Right on the cheek. Twice. Today, I smiled—inside and out.

ACCIDENTAL SEPARATION

One year, eight months

I've mentioned before that Matthew and Jonathan have rarely been apart. They've made separate trips to the grocery store a few times, but, with two older kids and a husband who works a lot, I just haven't had the time or the energy to intentionally separate them.

According to the experts out there, we are doing everything wrong.

So last night and this morning should have been emotionally traumatic for them. They should have cried for each other. They should have been looking around corners seeking each other out. They should been calling each other's names.

They didn't.

Last night, just before bed, Jonathan was walking through the living room when he somehow took an odd step and fell. He screamed and screamed and couldn't put weight on his left leg. So off we went to the ER while Matthew stayed behind with dad.

X-rays revealed no obvious fracture, but the doctor suspected injury to the soft tissue. I left Matthew behind again today to pick up the X-rays and stop by the pediatrician's office for a quick check of the circulation in the splinted leg. Tomorrow, Jonathan and I will spend an estimated two hours in the orthopedic unit at Children's Hospital, thirty minutes away.

There have been no sad good-byes and no overzealous reunions between Matthew and Jonathan. Neither had any trouble getting to sleep on his own last night. Neither seems annoyed or upset to have the other back in his midst.

Aside from logistical challenges presented by the splint, Matthew and Jonathan have fallen right back into their usual relationship patterns without missing a beat. They seem confident in their relationship. Confident and secure.

NO LONGER ENTIRELY IDENTICAL
One year, eight months

We can easily tell the boys apart now.

Jonathan and I spent two hours at Children's Hospital today. He broke his shin bone, a small fracture. The doctor said it is a common toddler injury. Orange seems to be his favorite color right now, so that's what he will wear for the next four weeks.

Matthew seems more affected by the cast than Jonathan. With no active playmate, his curiosity is in overdrive. Yesterday, he climbed on the dining room table, got stuck in a small space between the hutch and the wall and repeatedly tried to empty the silverware drawer. He imitates his brother by crawling on the floor and dragging one foot along.

It's going to be a long four weeks.

SO WHAT DO WE CALL THEM NOW?

One year, eight months

Apparently those folks who insist that Matthew and Jonathan are not identical might just be right. Maybe not now. But they might be right someday.

Scientists have known for years that identical twins can differ in their expression of genes due to environmental influences, such as diet. But it was always assumed that the basic DNA--the genetic framework--was precisely the same. A 2008 study of nineteen sets of adult identical twins has thrown them for a loop.

The study, conducted by geneticist Carl Bruder of the University of Alabama, found slight differences in DNA sequences in some sets. In one set of identical twins in Bruder's study, a genetic variation indicated the risk of leukemia in one twin. That particular twin did, indeed, suffer from the disease while the other did not.

You see, all of us are supposed to inherit a copy of each gene from each parent, but sometimes, something happens that causes us to have too many or too few. Scientists believe those variations might put us at risk for certain diseases such as AIDS, leukemia, autism or lupus. These differences are called copy number variations and they were just discovered a few years ago.

Previously, the assumption was that if any of these variations were found in one identical twin, they would be found in the other because the twins come from the same egg and share exactly the same DNA. This study throws that theory out the window.

What remains a mystery, however, is whether these variations occur in utero or as we age. Bruder suspects they come with age. Regardless, his findings mean studies of identical twins could be valuable in figuring out which genes are linked with certain diseases.

I'm not terribly worried about our twins and genetic diseases. We have no life-altering threats on either side of the family as far as I know. But the study raises another question in my world: If identicals are not truly identical, what do we call them now? Almost identical? Mostly identical? Sort of identical? Same-egg children?

Will I someday have to admit that those annoying people who stop me in the mall for the sole purpose of informing me that my twins are not identical simply because one has less fat in his cheeks are right?

TWINS DAYS

Twins Days, an annual celebration of twins held in Twinsburg, Ohio, is the largest gathering of twins and other multiples in the world. Held the first weekend in August, the event honors the founding of Twinsburg in 1817 by identical twins Aaron and Moses Wilcox.

The festival is open to all ages, and admission fees are minimal ($4 per person in 2017). Come on your own, come with your twin, come with your siblings, cousins or friends who are twins. All twins, regardless of zygosity, are welcome.

The festival was first held in 1976 and attracts about 2,000 sets of twins from all over the country and the world. It also attracts many members of the scientific community, who invite attending twins to take part in twin studies to determine the genetic or non-genetic basis of a wide range of human traits. Twins are usually compensated for participating.

READY TO RUN
One year, eight months

My seven-year-old daughter and I were at an outpatient clinic for Children's Hospital the other day when a man entered the physical therapy room with his two-year-old son. This little boy was meeting with a therapist in the other half of the room, which was divided by a curtain.

I watched as the boy fought with his therapist and his dad, both of whom insisted he walk. He didn't want to walk. He wanted to drag himself across the floor using his arms. The dad smiled at me and said, "He broke his leg. He got the cast off two weeks ago and he won't put any weight on it."

Thanks to his twin, Jonathan will probably never meet that therapist.

That little boy was an only child, according to the father. He didn't try to walk on his cast and his parents carried him everywhere. They didn't push him. Now they wish they had. The doctor told them that would have made all the difference. We haven't pushed Jonathan. We don't need to.

Moments ago, Jonathan ran across the living room in his hip-to-toe cast and leaped into his bean bag chair. He was imitating his twin brother, who was lying in his own chair, laughing and watching as Jonathan flew. Earlier today, Jonathan climbed the steps to his Little Tykes slide and slid down on his belly face-first. Again, he was imitating his twin, who was imitating their eight-year-old brother.

When Jonathan reached the bottom, he pulled himself up and did it again.

Jonathan walked the neighborhood for so long yesterday that he ripped right through my sock, the one I had pulled over his cast to protect his toes from the concrete. Fortunately, it was one of those socks that had lost its mate. No. Jonathan will not need therapy.

My guess is that on November twelfth, when that cast is sawed from his leg, Jonathan will step down from the table. Then he will walk right out the doors of Children's Hospital eagerly searching for his identical twin brother.

TWO WAYS TO PLAY

One year, eight months

Again and again I have read that identical twins eventually become shaped by their environments—differently shaped by their individual experiences and interactions. We have seen evidence of that in Matthew and Jonathan in the past few weeks.

Jonathan has always been a little more mellow than his brother, but his broken leg has emphasized that part of him. It is most obvious in the way he plays with the Little People's doll house, a toy they inherited from their siblings.

In those first few days, when he had not yet learned to walk on the cast, Jonathan discovered new things about that house. He discovered that he could do more than just open it up, lay it on its back and attempt to sit inside it. He began walking people through the door (cars too!), sitting people in chairs and laying them in the beds.

Meanwhile, his brother learned how to open all the drawers in the kitchen. Matthew also learned to slip his fingers through the cracks on locked cabinets and pull small things through. He learned to use stools, backpacks and diaper boxes to reach all kinds of things on countertops and dressers.

Then Jonathan became mobile on his cast, and even started to run. I thought Matthew would be distracted, his energy sources drained by brotherly wildness. Jonathan isn't all that fast, but he's pretty darned good. And he can jump and climb, too.

But it wasn't enough. Matthew still craves action. He walks or runs aimlessly. He "fake" cries in hopes that I will pick him up and flip him upside down. He tumbles on top of Jonathan when Jonathan is sitting quietly, playing with a car, some blocks or a baby doll. He goes nonstop.

Jonathan gets frustrated.

Jonathan enjoys the rough-housing, but he kind of likes playing quietly sometimes now. He still has his moments—I just caught him trying to dump a loaf of bread onto the kitchen floor—but he has learned the value of imaginative play.

Matthew has taught him how to reach things he never thought possible (Coffee cups set way back on counter tops are a favorite.). Now we can only hope that Jonathan will teach Matthew a thing or two (and I'll be able to relax and drink that coffee).

FASHION FIGHTS

One year, nine months

The boys have started fighting.

They've always squabbled a bit over toys and attention. But the all-out, screaming-crying-kicking-tantrum kind of stuff has only recently begun. And that kind of fighting they have reserved for clothes.

Yes, clothes.

Both Jonathan and Matthew seem to have an affection for yellow and/or orange shirts and they will do anything to get them. They will even try to pull them off each other, bowling each other over in the process.

I haven't read any studies on identical twins and clothing preferences. I can only hope that this is just a phase or that, at least, they will someday prefer colors that are a bit less fluorescent, like maybe blue or green.

TOGETHER FOR PRESCHOOL

One year, nine months

A teacher from the preschool my daughter attended handed me a waiting-list form the other day. She'll take the boys when they are old enough, she said. Both of them. I was, and continue to be, ecstatic.

The preschool is run by the county, primarily for children with special needs. The teacher has only four slots for typical kids in her class: two for girls; two for boys. If she takes Matthew and Jonathan, they will fill all her typical-boy slots.

Dominant education practice dictates she recommend separating the boys. Yet, she's happy to take them together. She believes me when I say that they will probably do better together and that they barely acknowledge each other when they play in large groups.

Her attitude is a relief and it gives me hope that as more studies are conducted on identical twins and separation, common sense and open minds will prevail. Several states have passed laws eliminating the mandatory separation policies of multiples in public schools, but the movement has a long way to go.

For now, there is help for parents who are facing that battle or who want to get a jump start before their kids reach school-age. Twins Law (www.twinslaw.com) is an organization founded by a woman who is determined to change the way school administrators and teachers think. Check it out.

HE SAID HIS NAME!

One year, nine months

I was frustrated. So frustrated. I had bought a full-length mirror and mounted it in the nursery, hoping the image of himself would finally inspire Jonathan to say his name. Instead, Jonathan stood before his reflection and said "Maaaatttt."

"No, no, no," I said, pointing to his brother. "That's Matt. You are Jon."

After a few rounds, Jonathan changed his response. Instead of calling himself "Matt," he actually pointed to his brother and then said Matthew's name. Further pressure only made Jonathan clam up. Well, that was progress.

I sighed.

Jonathan knew who he was. He always responded to his name, but he just couldn't bring himself to verbalize it. Maybe the letter J was just too hard. But I knew in my heart that wasn't the issue. Jonathan wanted Matt's name, just like he wanted Matt's yellow bear, Matt's crib and Matt's shoes. He had never said his name and he wasn't going to. So I gave up.

I started to walk away.

Then I stopped.

I stopped because as I glanced back at Jonathan, I saw a familiar grin. It was that mischievous grin, the grin that tells me something big is about to happen. "Maaaattt," he said, signaling toward his brother.

I approached him with caution.

"Yes. That's Matt, but who is this?" I asked, pointing at Jonathan's image. "Who is in the mirror?"

That grin grew. It grew bigger than I'd ever seen it before. Then suddenly it burst into a bright, startled face full of excitement, a look of comprehension and recognition that used every muscle in Jonathan's face.

"Jaaaah," he said. "Jaaaah."

Close enough.

I grabbed him and hugged him tight.

"Yes, yes," I said. "You are Jon."

THEY CAN SPEAK. THEY JUST DON'T

One year, eleven months

It's official.

The boys can hear and understand spoken language just fine. They use plenty of inflection. They know at least twenty animal sounds and say them clearly. They even know many of their letter sounds. Matthew and Jonathan can verbally communicate with others.

When they want to.

The trouble is that like many twins, particularly identical boys, they really don't want to most of the time. They use the smallest parcel of language possible to get their messages across and, at twenty-three months old, they still refuse to put two words together. Really refuse. They shake their heads "no."

"Twin language," the therapist wrote on the form in the evaluation room of the early invention program. They understand each other and have no urgent desire to please us grown-ups with their linguistic skills.

That's why they just stare at folks who try to get them to wave "hello" or "good-bye," yet they holler "bye-bye" and shut the door behind me when I take them to the sitter's (They love going there!) That's why they say only the first sound of so many words. That's why I am frequently puzzled when they open the fridge and ask for milk by some term they came up with entirely on their own.

No therapy necessary, she said. They will figure it out. But we really should teach them sign language if we want to lessen the frequency of tantrums as they struggle with the realization that this isn't going to work forever, she said.

The other therapists had a few things to say, too. Mostly, they wondered how we do it. The evaluation room was like a preschool, filled with countless cool toys and contraptions that drew Jonathan and Matthew like magnets.

But the force wasn't strong enough.

Within twenty minutes, they were grabbing clipboards, standing on chairs, stealing shoes and flipping through notebooks of the three blissfully ignorant therapists. Their antics earned Jonathan and Matthew a ranking of thirty-six months for gross motor skills and thirty-one months for fine motor skills.

They made it only to twenty-one months for adaptive motor skills because I have, thus far, refused to introduce the potty. "I'm not potty training them until they can at least say the word 'potty,'" I told the therapist.

"Okay," she said. "Here's the sign."

THE GAMES THEY PLAY

One year, eleven months

They are not even two yet. Not quite. I have a few weeks left, but it seems Matthew and Jonathan can't wait. They have moved beyond their innocent baby antics and are playing like devious preschoolers.

They have always interacted with each other. As newborns, we would place them on opposite ends of the crib, all swaddled in their receiving blankets. Fifteen minutes later, we would find them in the middle of the crib, side-by-side with blankets undone and heads touching. By four months, old, the grunting had begun. They were like tiny caveman, exchanging grunts and giggles. People stared and most smiled.

Games of chase came with toddlerhood. Shouts of "Go, go, go," from one twin would trigger laps through the kitchen, dining room and living room with one toddler fast on the heels of the other. They even set up obstacle courses of sorts and took turns completing them.

The most popular went like this: Lie down and kick the safety gate; run to the recliner and slap hands on the leather (laugh); run over to the pillow they had thrown on the floor in just the right spot and jump. Laugh like crazy and start over.

They were amazing in their creativity, and we were proud.

But, in the past few weeks, they have taken their level of play up a few notches. And it's all about games. There is the usual stuff: tag, wrestling, cheering each other on as they run and leap into their bean bag chairs. Then there are the creative games: beg mom to let them color, "accidentally" throw a crayon on the floor, wait for her to pick it up and then pelt her with orange, green, blue and pink as she squats; grab sippy cups and dance with them, chanting, "aye, aye, aye," which, for some reason, makes them each laugh so hard, they can't breathe; "set" the table when mom isn't looking; set up Hot Wheel tracks all by themselves by sticking one end into the sofa and creating a ramp.

If that's not enough, they have both developed the cackle. A cackle that says, "Hee, hee! We've just pulled one over on mom. Let's watch her turn red and growl when she sees it!"

Ugh! My babies didn't do this.

The worst part about this new phase of theirs is that I get absolutely nothing done. Not a thing. And it's not because they are into everything, moving nonstop and fearless. Rather, I get no work done because I can't stop watching. I am amazed by these devious and creative toddlers.

Stunned and amazed.

HALFWAY TO FOUR

Two years

I feel like I should write something profound for their second birthday. Something poetic, insightful, and wondrously quotable. It has, after all, been a monumental year for Matthew and Jonathan. They learned to walk. They learned to talk. They exchanged bottles for sippy cups. They even learned that they are separate entities—that Matt is Matt and Jon is Jon.

Every day, their maturity and the skills that come with it enable Matthew and Jonathan to give us more and more glimpses into the people they are and the people they will become. Yet, as we celebrated their birthday yesterday, I found I couldn't do it. I couldn't write about those things.

All I could think about, honestly, was that two is halfway to four and that by four, they will be potty trained, they will respond to reason at some level, they will no longer need a stroller and they will talk in sentences.

That doesn't mean I want to rush them. No, not at all. I don't want them to grow up too fast. I adore their little kisses on my lips, cheeks and nose. I long for their tiny hands around my neck. I cherish their nonsensical exchanges that result in fits of giggles.

And, wow. That unconditional trust only babies and toddlers have. That belief that mom is all-powerful, all-knowing, all-everything. That she is flawless. I see that in their eyes as they reach for me. They believe that I can make anything better. They really do.

No, I don't want to rush through that.

But they exhaust me lately as much as they exhilarate me. And I find the exhaustion much easier to contend with if I have something to look forward to. So, on their birthday, while I was chasing them around the house trying desperately to persuade them to keep their clothes and diapers on at least until our neighbors arrived for cake and ice cream, I focused on the future.

I focused on how much easier it will become instead, thinking about how hard it sometimes has been. With that in mind, I found I could laugh at our little strippers and I caught them. They made it through the evening fully clothed.

CRUCIAL PRODUCTS FOR GUYS LIKE MINE

Two years

Something tugged at me the other night, pulling me toward the nursery and urging me to check on Matthew and Jonathan. I hate to do that. So often, it wakes them. But this feeling was so strong, that I opened the doors anyway. And when I did, I found Matthew asleep underneath his fitted crib sheet.

It frightened me, but it did not surprise me.

These guys are clever, curious and determined. A few days earlier, I had come into the nursery during nap time to find both boys shouting and giggling with their legs tucked underneath the sheets. They had figured out how to reach down the sides of the mattresses, grab the elastic from underneath and pull the sheets up.

That first incident gave me a little time to research the options.

I knew straps wouldn't work, not the way they were doing this. I had to find something that would make their sheets immobile. It took a few hours and a lot of creative Internet searches, but I finally found the solution. Four Secure-Fit crib sheets from Halo Innovations arrived via Federal Express Ground today. I took them out of the package and smiled. This company knows my boys.

The arrival of the sheets got me thinking about the items I have found invaluable to high-energy, creative twin boys. And I'd like to share a few of my favorites. No one has paid me or influenced me in any way in exchange for these endorsements.

Let's start with the sheets:

Halo Secure-Fit crib sheets: These sheets have deep pockets on either end to keep the sheets on. One side slips over the mattress. The other side Velcros into place. Parents of multiples can get discounts by calling customer service number.

Halo Big Kid's Sleep Sack Wearable Blanket: These are essential for children like mine who are climbers and they are much easier to use than crib nets. The larger sleep sacks have foot hole so toddlers can stand and walk, but they can't lift their legs over the sides of cribs.

Podee Hands Free Baby Bottles: What can I say about these? They brought me sanity once I stopped nursing. Podee bottles have a long, flexible tube that leads to a nipple and reaches far down to the bottom of the bottle. Parents can push a stroller through a mall with bottles tucked in at their twins' sides and nipples in mouths. With two older kids who needed my attention and lots of events to attend outside the home, these were crucial for me. They kept everyone happy. It beats propping bottles or listening to one baby scream while the other eats.

Step2 Safari Wagon: This wagon has a deep leg well for tall toddlers like mine and seat belts to contain them. It also has an easily removable roof with cup holders for my coffee. One of the seats lifts for storage. The boys have holders for their sippy cups or snacks. I no longer see the Safari model for sale on their site. The closest is the Canopy Wagon, which appears to be the same product minus the sippy cup holder.

Baby Trend Snap-N-Go double stroller: This saved my back in those early months. The frame is light-weight and works with most brands of infant car seats. You just lift the car seat out of the vehicle, snap it into the frame and go. The basket underneath has plenty of room, too. Unfortunately, my very-tall boys outgrew their infant seats by five months.

Starbucks: Drive-thru, drink-in, brew-at-home. I don't know how I would have made it through the first two years without Starbucks.

TWO-YEAR STATS
Two years

Not all identical twins develop identically in their physical growth.

Just last week, I met identical twin girls at the local mall with their mom. The girls were three years old and one was more than an inch taller than the other. The difference, the mom said, was likely caused by twin-to-twin transfusion syndrome, a condition in which one twin is deprived of nutrients from a shared placenta. TTTS forced doctors to deliver them at twenty-seven weeks or lose the smaller twin.

Our guys were lucky.

Each had his own sac and his own placenta. Their placentas were on polar-opposite sides of the uterus. It can't get better or safer than that. Their placement in utero was so unusual that it took DNA tests to persuade my OB that they are, indeed, identical. So I wasn't surprised by the findings at their two-year physical:

Height: Both boys are thirty-seven and one half inches tall, landing them off the charts compared to other boys their age. Our two older children are off the charts for height as well. It's in their genes. Their dad looms ten inches above me at six feet, five inches tall.

Head: Their measurements were precisely the same even though most folks insist that Jonathan's head is bigger. Jonathan has slightly more fat in his cheeks than his brother. I sometimes wonder if that is because Jonathan was born via cesarean section while Matthew experienced a vaginal birth. It's not likely, but it's something to think about.

Weight: Matthew was the lighter of the two at thirty-one pounds, four ounces. Jonathan weighed in at exactly thirty-two pounds. It might be the cheek fat. It might have been a wet diaper. It might have been because Matthew takes so much more pleasure in throwing his food than in eating it. Who knows?

Overall, the doctor proclaimed Jonathan and Matthew healthy, but she referred them to specialists for speech and hearing. Though the county program proclaimed them on track, she felt their reluctance to use more than one syllable per word and their refusal to put to words together is probably the source of unnecessary frustration.

She figures twinese is the cause, but that a little therapy might make life better for all of us. I have to agree. So, off we go to Children's Hospital. We'll be checking back with the pediatrician in six months. Hopefully, by then, we'll be asking for advice on how to tune out their constant chatter.

DOUBLE TIME-OUTS: THE LOGISTICS

Two years

When one twin commits a wrong, the other often has to try it for himself seconds later. So what do you do? How do you give toddler twins simultaneous time-outs when sitting still for any length of time under any circumstances is a challenge?

Here's how I do it:

I squat down, grab both boys and sit on my heels. I pull one twin on each knee and, for each child, I bring one of my arms over his shoulder and diagonally across his chest like a seat belt. Then I grab one of his thighs and he is locked in.

He can't get out.

I very awkwardly place my head between theirs so that if they thrash about, their heads will hit my cheeks instead of each other's skulls. Then I count to two minutes in my head and pray that my arms will hold out.

When it's over, they both get a reminder, a hug and kiss.

It took some time, but they are finally learning that I am stronger, more clever and more determined than they are. More often these days I am doing one time-out at a time. They are even learning to sit for the duration with only occasional repositioning. (Well, okay, every fifteen seconds or so.).

1-2-3 MAGIC

The twins were four when I discovered this book. How I wish I'd read it sooner. The title can be misleading. I ignored the book for years despite multiple recommendations, thinking it was just some self-proclaimed expert expounding on the obvious value of counting to three when transitioning activities. But that's not what it's about at all. *1-2-3 Magic*, by clinical psychologist Thomas W. Phelan, is a three-step method of discipline for kids ages 2 to 12.

It works.

TWINS ARE DANGEROUS

Two years

Twins are dangerous, especially at two years old.

I concluded that today when I realized that I couldn't do dishes with fresh cuts on three of my knuckles on my right hand. Only one injury was new, but the other two had occurred within the past twenty-four hours and had reopened during the last incident.

All three can be blamed on the twins.

The first knuckle scratch happened when I was trying to scoop food up from underneath the dining room table. The twins had tossed their lunch freely throughout the dining room, a favorite game of theirs. I was hurrying because Jonathan was anxious to squish the very-soft green beans into the floorboards. I turned a bit too quickly and hit my head. As I reached for my head, I scraped my knuckle on the rough wood under the table.

The second incident was diaper-related. I was reaching for a diaper in the cabinet above the changing table while trying to keep Matthew from kicking me. He does that when he prefers nakedness and I insist on clothing. Just as my hand grasped the diaper, I got a foot in my stomach. I yanked my right hand back and scraped the knuckle on the cabinet door.

The third incident occurred this morning. Both boys had stripped while I was in the bathroom. I found Matthew leaning causally against the sofa while peeing on the carpet. I rushed to get him on a potty and spied Jonathan peeing on the hardwood by the front door. It was too late for Matthew anyway, so I put him down and grabbed some paper towel, hoping to at least soak up some of Jonathan's mess before anyone slid in it. As I passed Matthew, he started peeing again.

I threw my arms out in exasperation and caught my knuckles on the edge of the counter top, creating a new cut and reopening the other two. To make matters worse, I have a Band-Aid on my fingertip. That incident was unrelated. I was trying to re-cork a bottle of wine and cut my finger on some remaining foil.

But wait. Why did I drink that red wine last night? Oh yeah, the twins. See what I mean?

Twins are dangerous.

I JUST KNEW

Two years, one month

It happened for the first time yesterday and I'm having trouble containing my excitement. I was uploading images from our digital camera onto the computer when I saw a photo of one of the boys. My first thought—my very first and very confident thought—was that's Jonny! Moments later, it happened again, this time in a photo of the boys together. I immediately recognized Matty on the right.

Now, I know I sound like a horrible mother, so I should say that I have always been able to figure out who is who in photos eventually. I look at their clothes, at the toys in their hands, at the food on their faces. Sometimes, I have to squint a little and study the blue veins on the bridges of their noses (thick, Jonathan; thin, Matthew). With time, I can identify them.

But this was different. This time I just knew. Right away. Immediately. I've never been so instantly sure. And I know why. Matthew and Jonathan are growing up and as they grow, their personalities are beginning to break through in a physical way—even in photos. In one photo I looked at yesterday, Jonathan offers an expression that belongs only to him, a sort of puppy-eyed, pleading look. Matthew has become a ham with cameras. He scrunches his face into a funny little smile and tilts his head up, like he did in another photo I viewed.

I couldn't help myself. I picked up the camera and started shooting more.

A DIFFERENT KIND OF MOM

Two years, one month

I used to be a better mom.

My kids, my older kids, never had more than two hours a day of combined screen time (television and computer) as per the recommendations of the American Academy of Pediatrics. Even then, I allowed only commercial-free television and educational computer games.

I scoffed at moms who regularly visited McDonald's or Burger King. Once a month was too much in my opinion. I shopped for fruit and vegetables at a local produce store and dessert was a rarity.

Doughnuts? Forget it.

The house was clean. The kids were in bed by eight p.m. My children were well-disciplined, knowing that time-outs would come swiftly—anytime, anywhere—if they misbehaved. I was in tune with them, responding to their every whimper.

Now they have to scream.

The twins had their first McDonald's French fries before they turned a year old (They don't like the nuggets.). The television is on often. Sometimes, I just pray that they'll actually watch it so I can have a break.

At least once a day, I pretend not to see an infraction because I don't have the energy for a time-out. I know it will come back to haunt me in the long run, but I don't think as far in advance as I used to. I just hope that I'll get through each day.

I lose my temper with the older kids quickly if they argue. On the weekends, they get far more computer time than they should. They went to bed at nine-thirty last night, a school night, because my husband was sick and I had too much to do before I could get around to their bedtime routine.

I was feeling horrible about my new parenting methods as I prepared, at midnight, to finally drag myself up to bed. Then I picked up the snack dishes the older kids had left behind and I smiled. Riley, who just celebrated his ninth birthday, had asked for spinach as part of his snack. Not a leaf was left behind. His seven-year-old sister, Kiersten, had asked for a cheese stick. Granted, they'd had two small cookies, but it never occurred to them to ask for more.

I'd had good conversations with each as I read to them and tucked them in. They had cleaned their rooms when I asked, showered when I asked and turned the TV off when I told them to. Earlier in the evening, they had come into the nursery to give their twin brothers goodnight kisses. Jonathan and Matthew had grinned in delight at the sight of their older siblings, who share a bond not much unlike their own.

As I turned off lights, removed books from beds and shut bedroom doors, I couldn't help thinking that Riley and Kiersten have not been "ruined" by a few too many hours of television or computer time. Nor have they been destroyed by an occasional doughnut on a Wednesday morning. And I think I know why.

The one thing that has not changed is that we all listen. We listen to each other with respect and caring and love, even when we're angry or frustrated or overwhelmed or when we need to take a few minutes to ourselves first. Maybe the rest is overrated. Maybe there is hope for the twins.

THE NURSING GAME:
I'M NOT PLAYING ANYMORE

Two years, two months

I was at Cincinnati's Children's Museum with the twins last week when another twin mom tried to engage me in the nursing game. I don't like the nursing game. It's not fun and these moms only goad me into playing it because they know they will win. It starts bluntly like this:

"Your boys are so big! Did you nurse them?"

What?

Does breast milk include huge doses of growth hormone? Their dad is six-foot-five. Their brother and sister are way off the charts for height. So why shouldn't the twins be tall, too? Then again, my husband and both older kids were nursed as babies.

Hmmm.

I stupidly make the next move. I don't know why. Boredom maybe. I am often aching for adult conversation.

"Yes. I did."

"Oh really? For how long?"

"Four months."

«Oh.»

I don't explain. And that complicates the game. She's stuck—unless she plays the formula-is-so-expensive-thank-goodness-I-never-had-to-use-it-because-I-nursed-my-twins-exclusively-for,-like,-two-years card.

I am fortunate, though. One of her twins takes off and she's off like a shot with him, the other twin in tow. The boys and I wander elsewhere and I don't see her again. But I'm tired of the game and I don't want to play anymore. So I've decided to show my cards once and for all.

Yes. I nursed my older kids. My son gave up on me at eight months. He had better things to do and really resented the time it took to nurse. He preferred a bottle even though I made him drink it on my lap.

My daughter nursed for fifteen months and showed no signs of quitting. Then she fell on the tile near the fireplace and sliced her tongue with her teeth. She couldn't nurse for several days and, finally, made her transition to cups. I felt terrible for her, but I also felt that she'd had a darned good run.

When the twins were born, I was determined to nurse them, too. I shouldn't deny them, I said to myself, simply because they happened to be born at the same time. It wouldn't be fair. And, of course, I thought it would be a breeze. I was a breastfeeding veteran.

But Matthew and Jonathan both had trouble latching when they were born, identical troubles. I spent ten frustrating days nursing, bottle feeding and then pumping with barely an hour's break before I had to start all over again.

When they finally did latch (on the same day at about the same time), they still had their issues. Matthew would grab on and go to town for ten minutes straight. Then he'd quit. That was it. No more no matter how hungry he seemed to be.

Jonathan would take a full ten minutes to get latched. Then he would nurse endlessly and scream if I tried to take him off. He was a slow nurser. For some reason, it took a great deal of effort for him. It was stressful. And school added to the stress.

My daughter attended half days and my son attended full days. I had no help during the day or when my husband travelled and we lived nowhere near family. Poor Matthew and Jonathan were often rushed through nursings so I could get the older kids to school. Later, they were rushed to the bus stop or the gymnasium to pick the older kids up. After that, we often had dance or Cub Scouts.

I tried pumping, but I had even less time for that. And the stress took its toll. I was lucky to get two or four ounces when I pumped and I sometimes pumped for an hour straight. The only time I could nurse the boys comfortably was during those few hours in the afternoon when both older kids were in school. I lived for those moments. It was peaceful. It was pleasant.

Most of the time.

Okay, hardly ever, but sometimes and sometimes was good enough. Most often, both boys would cry with hunger at the same time and I wasn't good at tandem nursing. I was too big when I nursed (a quadruple D I'd say, if there is such a thing) and it was terribly uncomfortable for all three of us. Someone had to cry while the other ate. So I started using formula, a few ounces here and a few ounces there, more and more.

After three months, I was such a mess that I knew I had to make a decision.

Nothing beats breast milk, but I had the health of the family as a whole to consider. So, one month later, the day school ended, I nursed Matthew and Jonathan for the last time. I ought to reflect on the sadness of that moment, but I can't. While I'll admit I felt some guilt, the overwhelming emotion was relief. Immense and intense relief.

There.

Game over.

IDENTICAL TWINS, FRATERNAL EATERS

One year, two months

Our oldest son is vegetarian. He is nine and hasn't eaten meat in five years. Our seven-year-old daughter makes up for her brother's lack of meat consumption. She routinely eats the meat, fruit and vegetables and she leaves the carbs behind. She'll even leave French fries untouched.

I have always figured their eating habits were genetically influenced. After all, our oldest two children are only seventeen months apart and they were raised in the same eating environment. I can't imagine what we might have done that would have made such a drastic difference in their eating habits. But the twins defy my logic.

The other day, I tried an experiment. I gave the boys hot dogs, PB&J, cheese and green beans for lunch. As expected, Matthew ate all of his hot dog and most of Jonathan's. He had seconds and thirds on green beans. He had one bite of PB&J and none of the cheese.

Jonathan ate two bites of hot dog. He ate all of his PB&J and polished off Matthew's. He ate his own cheese and his brother's and then asked for more. He had seconds on the green beans, but didn't finish his second serving.

Matthew ate the meat and lots veggies. Jonathan ate the carbs, non-meat protein and a moderate amount of veggies. This is the pattern that has been developing over the past few months. I don't get it. The twins have the same DNA. They have always been offered the same foods at the same times. I would expect some differences in their eating habits; Even though they are identical twins, they are different people with minds and preferences of their own.

But this goes beyond that. They are emulating the opposite habits of their older brother and sister. That might make sense if they were around them more often. But, thanks to school, the four children usually eat only dinner together. And at dinner, our oldest son eats what we eat with either beans, or a soy- or whey-based product as a meat substitute. They don't see his PB&Js or her rolled up salami.

I just don't get it.

THEIR VOICES EMERGE
Two years, three months

They are speaking.

Really, really speaking and, wow, is it cool.

It all started just after their second birthday, the day I picked up the phone to make the appointment with a speech therapist. I got distracted and planned to call again later. Suddenly, I heard, "Bye, bye, truck."

And it just poured out from there.

Three months ago, Matthew and Jonathan would not string two words together. The single words they used were mostly one-syllable words and they often would leave off the ending sounds. I tried not to worry. Many online friends with identical boys of similar ages were experiencing the same delays.

The county folks who had evaluated Matthew and Jonathan said they communicated in all other ways, and that they had simply fallen into the habits of twinese or twin language. They entertained each other and had no desire to please adults with their speaking abilities. The county team suggested sign language, but assured me that Matthew and Jonathan would eventually come around.

Our pediatrician recommended a few therapy sessions anyway to encourage them to speak and to help ease the frustrations that bring about so many tantrums when children grow intellectually, but are still not able to communicate their needs and desires. This was the appointment I was trying to make that day in January.

Now my concerns seem silly.

I was in the kitchen this morning when I heard, "Ready, set, go!" from foyer. Then around the corner came Matthew in the lead with the smaller toy shopping cart. Jonathan was at his heels, with the larger one, laughing like crazy. When I told them they needed to get dressed, Jonathan said "Shirt? Pants?" and went right for the dresser. He picked up a blue shirt with a ball and net on front and said, "Basketball? Shirt on?" clear as day.

The boys can count to ten. They know their colors. They know the alphabet and most of the letter sounds. They say, "One, two, three. Green!" when we stop at a red light.

This morning, as we headed out the door for a three-hour visit to the sitter, Matthew said, "Cole's house?" And that was exactly where we were headed, to the home of our three-year-old neighbor Cole and his nanny, who cares for Matthew and Jonathan two mornings each week. I answered him and the three of us—Matthew, Jonathan and I—had a little conversation about Cole and his little sister and their toy dinosaurs.

We actually had a conversation.

It was so cool.

A CLOSER LOOK

Two years, four months

It's strange and, maybe, it's just a phase, but I find that I rarely think of Matthew and Jonathan as identical twins these days.

All I can figure is that I am so focused on the intimate, complex achievements that come with this age, that I am unable to step back and see them from any kind of distance anymore. Their recent developments have given me the opportunity to see the minutia and, in the minutia, I see two little people who are so very different from each other.

For instance, language has given them the tools to verbally express their individuality, like Jonathan and his obsession with Swiper the Fox from the children's show *Dora the Explorer*, an obsession that Matthew does not share:

«Swiper?»

«Fox?»

«Sneaky?»

"Naughty?"

«Oh man!»

(Repeat ten times and insist mom repeat each word as affirmation that she is listening.)

Or Matthew with his bathing preferences, preferences that Jonathan clearly does not share: "No toys!" Matthew shrieks as a small zebra, a cup and a teething ring come flying out of the bathtub. Jonathan stands, reaches in vain for the discarded playthings and then throws his hands up and cries.

"Toys done," Matthew says triumphantly. "No toys!"

Improved mobility and agility have given them the skills to individually test their physical limits while also applying the techniques of observation and manipulation. For instance, Matthew has learned to appear fully absorbed in play in their fenced-in area out back, leaving me with a sense of security as I try to sneak inside for a moment to unload the dishwasher. As soon as my back is turned, he is over the fence and around the front of the house. Jonathan remains fenced in, too awed to throw a leg over and follow.

Jonathan, meanwhile, is focused on his jumping skills. He arranges bean bag chairs a few feet away from the sofa and then, calculating the distance just perfectly, he leaps from the sofa into the bean bag chairs face-first.

Greater reasoning ability, empathy and perspective has given them both the skills to manipulate their environment and the people in it to their liking.

A few examples:

Matthew will turn my head in his direction with his tiny hands, cock his own head in the cutest little way, scrunch his eyes just right and say, "Cars? Watch Cars?" He knows he makes my heart melt. He knows I can't resist. In goes the Cars DVD.

Jonathan keeps one eye on his brother and waits for that moment when Matthew wants to cuddle with me. Then he runs over, pushes his twin brother aside, climbs into my arms and declares, "Mine! Mine!" As soon as Matthew loses interest in the battle for attention, Jonathan slips off my lap and resumes play.

Matthew climbs onto the sofa, lays his head on a pillow and covers himself with a blanket, just like his older brother does each morning when he first wakes up. And then, in his desire to complete the charade, he says, "Ovaltine? Ovaltine?" requesting his idol's favorite drink and hoping it gets his attention.

Sometimes, when I am crouched down, picking raisins off the floor, scrubbing milk out of the carpet or scooping up bits of crushed crackers, I'll feel two perfect hands tickle my neck and Jonathan will be standing right in front of me. He'll say, "love!" and then kiss me right on the lips. Just as he predicts, I stop what I'm doing and cradle this amazing human being.

It was a lot easier when the twins were more like a unit, when I could step back and say this is who "they" are, this is what "they" do, how "they" behave. Still, I wouldn't ever want to be positioned so far away again. This new phase is exhausting, but it's also exhilarating. I am finally getting the chance to know them, to know them as individuals. As Matthew and Jonathan, brothers who just happen to both be two.

IDENTICAL TWINS AND HEREDITY
Two years, three months

The question came up again on an online forum. And, once again, folks hopped into the discussion with both feet, readily giving incomplete and misleading answers with confidence. The question? Can the tendency to have identical twins be inherited? The most common answer and the prevailing theory is "no."

Most OBs will tell their patients that identical twins are fluke, an accident of nature, and that their chances of having another set are no greater than any other woman's chance of having identicals in the first place. But how does that explain my neighbor's daughter and her family? She has three sets of identical twin boys who come trick-or-treating to our house every year.

And what about the woman whose daughter took dance lessons with my daughter? She is an identical twin and she has identical twin boys of her own. Then there is the woman I met at a local bakery. She looked longingly at my boys (who were screaming at my attempt to get some coffee, unwilling to be pacified by cookies) and told me that her two daughters each have a set of identical twin girls.

It just doesn't make sense.

The reality is that scientists have no idea why some women have identical twins and some don't. Evidence does exist that many sets are flukes. For instance, there is no history in my family or in my husband's family of identical twins, as far as we know.

My side boasts a set of twins and a set of triplets way back in the olden days, but they were fraternal. My mother-in-law remembers a set of triplets birthed by a distant relative, but they also were fraternal. So our boys probably were an accident of nature, an awesome accident. But in other families, the frequency is too great for simple coincidence. The journalist in me demanded that I do some research.

This is what I found:

A 2007 study, led by Dr. Dianna Payne, a visiting research fellow at the Mio Fertility Clinic in Japan, shows identical twins form just after conception when an embryo collapses and splits in two. She discovered this by photographing growing embryos every two minutes in a lab using special computer software.

Her evidence negates previously held theories that the egg splits after it leaves its shell immediately before implantation, and that identical twins, therefore, either shared a placenta or had individual placentas that grew close together. The predominance of the previous theory explains why my OB insisted that our boys were fraternal until they were DNA tested. Our boys each had their own placentas, which grew on polar opposite side of my uterus. They were born in January of 2007, just before Dr. Payne and her colleagues went public with their research.

Dr. Payne's discovery has opened new paths for research into the potential genetic impact on identical twinning. A study is currently underway that proposes a male enzyme is involved. Scientists already know the enzyme causes the embryo to collapse, but they are unsure who secretes it or why. The study, as far as I know, is not yet public.

But I found a post—written by a graduate bioengineering student who is helping to conduct the study at an unnamed university—on a Yahoo forum (http://www.twinslist.org/idfaq.htm). The poster says the study also suggests some women carry a gene that prevents the enzyme from splitting the egg, and that men who produce the enzyme do not produce it every time:

"Thus far, the research shows that the enzyme is directly responsible for causing the splitting of the chromosomes, which results in the division of the cytoplasm which results in two eggs! There are a few (about 1%) that have alluded us so far and have shown no sign of the enzyme despite the fact that twins resulted. Thus, we have concluded that identical twinning can also be a random event. But in about 99% of the people tested, the enzyme is apparently the culprit. So, 99% is a darn good yield! So, according to our research, it is not a small percentage but almost the entire percentage."

This part of the post explains why we know so little:

"And yes, this study has been repeated already, but very, very little money is put into this research, so most of it is done on our own time. The reason for this is there is little to no medical advances that can come out of the research, just info and most of the money on medical and genetic research is for improving the outcome of diseases, etc. So, that is why it may be a while before this research is completed. We have to get about 5% of the public who have twins to complete our research (not all will go through tests, some will just answer questionnaires) before we can say that this represents the entire population, so you can see that this will take a while!"

So that's it.

The answer is that there is no definitive answer because the people in medical community, or rather the folks who fund their research, are just not all that interested. For now, the influences on identical twinning remain a mystery.

IDENTICAL VOICES, FRATERNAL INFLECTIONS

Two years, three months

Matthew and Jonathan have the same cry.

When I hear them call out over the monitor at night, I can never tell whether the same toddler has awakened twice or whether both woke up at different times. It drives me crazy, especially when they are sick. So, before they started speaking, I often wondered whether they would have the same voice. I finally have my answer.

They do.

But they don't.

If both boys say the same thing with the same inflection (and they often do), their voices are indistinguishable from one another. They also have a similar vocabulary and are at the same stage of speech development. They string words together, but they do not form complete sentences. What distinguishes them in speech is not their voices, but their personalities.

Matthew likes to yell.

Sometimes, he'll just stand there and holler, "Mom! Mom!" in a flat, loud, determined tone even though I'm right there. Then he'll grin. He just really loves to yell. It seems to makes him feel good, strong, in control. If he wants to go into the basement playroom, he commands me: "Mom! Basement!"

Jonathan doesn't do that.

When I hear a question asked in soprano, that's when I know it's Jonathan speaking. He is inquisitive and his voice often climbs almost unbearably high when he struggles with that first syllable of a question. When Jonathan wants to play in the basement, I hear a high-pitched squeak that grows louder, stronger and fuller as it finally escapes: "Basement?"

He doesn't command me; He makes an appeal to me.

Over time, I'm sure experience will change their approaches. They will learn, like we all do, how people react to their attempts to manipulate with intonation and inflection, and their voices will be like their cries. They will be indistinguishable.

But that's okay.

That's okay because, by then, I won't need to hear different voices to know who is speaking. Jonathan and Matthew will have different interests, different concerns, different questions, different life experiences. Their personalities will override their biological similarities. They will sound different simply because they are different.

SOMETIMES IT WOULD BE NICE IF THEY ACTED LIKE TWINS

Two years, four months

I had to laugh the other day when I thought about all those parents who fret about separating their identical twins in school, or who dress their twins in assigned colors only, or who enroll them in different activities regardless of their interests—all with the goal of promoting individuality.

I had to laugh because individuality is the reason I need a mother's helper one day a week this summer. Individuality is the reason I had to order two more yellow shirts from Children's Place last week. Individuality is the reason we have huge battles at bath time these days. And I can't recall doing anything specific to promote it.

For instance, I can't take Matthew and Jonathan to any public place that is not fenced in by myself because as soon as I set them down, they run off in opposite directions. They might nod at each other occasionally, but rarely do they interact at all. They are content in the knowledge that the other is there and, for some reason, that contentment gives them confidence. And energy.

So, if I want to take the older kids to the zoo, the Museums Center or the splash park, I need another pair of hands. My mother's helper is fourteen years old. She is our neighbor's daughter. She was so excited when she accepted the job. She was so exhausted after our trip to the zoo on Wednesday. I hope she has the strength to last another eight weeks.

I had to buy those yellow shirts (on sale, thank goodness) because that's all Matthew will wear lately. Jonathan will wear only orange, though both are willing to make an exception for red or green shirts once in a while as long as we are willing to endure an amazingly long and loud tantrum first. Jonathan will wear only shorts no matter how cool it is outside. Matthew will wear only pants no matter how hot it is outside. And bath time. Bath time has turned into a disaster. Jonathan wants bubbles and toys. Matthew wants clear water and no toys.

I'm finding I can ease the resulting aggression by grabbing a few cars from their toy bin and throwing those in the water. Matthew doesn't view the cars as "bath toys." Jonathan does. So, until the novelty wears off, I'm saved once again.

THE BIG-BOY BED DISASTER

Two years, four months

We finally made the move and it's been horrible.

Matthew and Jonathan are in big boy beds.

I was hoping to keep them in cribs until they turned eighteen, but nothing was working anymore. We'd brought the crib mattresses down as low as they could go and we clothed them in big-kid sleep sacks, but still, they managed. They managed so well that I found Jonathan perched on the highest wall of his crib the other day at nap time and I watched, unable to reach him on time, as he leaped into Matthew's crib.

It was terrifying.

So I bought beds and had them set up within five hours. But these two feed off each other. Their similar temperaments mean they are similarly wild. In their cribs, they jumped up and down simultaneously until they simply couldn't do it anymore and they crashed. In their beds, they do the same thing except now there are no crib rails to confine them.

Now, they jump off the beds, or leap from one bed to the other. Now, they get out of bed, open dresser drawers, climb them and pull their lullaby CD from its player. Now, they dump laundry out of the basket and scatter it all over the floor. Now, they don't nap and it's draining to put them to bed at night.

We tried lying down with them. (We can spare only one person at a time because we do, after all, have two older kids.) They step on our tummies, our faces, our legs. When we focus on settling one into bed, the other twin makes a beeline for the door.

We tried putting them down every time they got up without saying a word. That worked with our older kids. The older kids gave up after they realized they weren't going to get attention for their antics. Not so with these guys. They get giggles out of each other. And that's enough attention for them. So now we shut them in like prisoners.

We built a high gate for the door that will keep them in, but allow us to see and hear them. We give them some toys, listen for any sounds of true disaster and pray that they will be okay. When all is quiet, we go in and pick them up off the floor or straighten their little bodies on their beds, and change their diapers. Then we cover them up and shut the door only to find them standing in those dresser drawers again as soon as we hear the first peep over the monitor in the morning.

Yes, the dresser is attached to the wall, but it might loosen. It might give way. Yes, they eventually fall asleep at night, but they wake at the crack of dawn and, without naps, their personalities are not so pleasant anymore. My "good-natured terrors" are losing their good natures. Yes, we should consider separate rooms for naps, but we don't have the space right now and we definitely don't have the childproofed space.

So, I guess all I can do for now is keep trying to get them to bed even earlier, duct-tape the dresser drawers every night and have patience. Have patience that the days will grow shorter again and they will sleep longer. Have patience that as they get older, they will need less sleep. Have patience that their good natures will once again take over. But first, I have to figure out how to find that patience.

POTTY TRAINING: WHERE ONE GOES, THE OTHER WILL FOLLOW

Two years, five months

Jonathan has always let Matthew take the lead in all things physical.

When Matthew was learning to crawl, Jonathan sat aloof, unmoving, in the center of the living room floor and watched. He watched for weeks as Matthew learned to fall from sitting position onto his belly, lift himself up onto his hands and knees, rock back and forth, and then, finally, propel his body in different directions. Two days later, Jonathan was at least as fast as his brother. It was the same scenario for rolling over, sitting up and walking.

So I supposed I shouldn't be surprised that Jonathan shows no interest in potty training while Matthew is obsessed. It started at the sitter's three days ago and Matthew's obsession has grown each day since. This morning, he refused all potty seats and the toilet insert. Instead, he propped himself up on the big toilet and, for almost two hours, he sat and peed and sat and peed, watching *Once Upon a Potty* over and over.

He missed a few times and he didn't quite get there for number two (though he knew it was coming and he tried), but he had three or four successes (He drinks a lot.). Meanwhile, his brother sat on the sofa, aloof and unmoving, drinking milk.

For a moment, I thought Jonathan might join in. He stood up, pulled off his shorts and peeled off his diaper with an eager look on his face. I pointed him toward a potty seat and he moved forward, right past it to the Cars pull-up on the floor next to it. He handed me the pull-up and his shorts and said, "Cars? On?"

So I helped Jonathan into his pull-up, gave him more milk and turned back to Matthew, who was alternating toilet-flushing with toilet-sitting and hand-washing. Matthew was, once again, taking on the physical burden for his identical twin.

But he didn't seem to mind and, although Jonathan's eyes appeared glued to the little cartoon Joshua who was sitting on a little cartoon potty, I'm sure I saw his eyes shift to the bathroom every now and then. So, for now, I'll focus on teaching Matthew. And I'll let the brothers work out the rest.

MORE THAN TWINS: FRIENDS

Two years, five months

One day several weeks ago, Jonathan took me by the hand and pulled. "Come on, Mom," he said, leading me toward the room he shares with Matthew. "Come on. Play." And I did. This method of manipulation was new to Jonathan and he was thrilled that it had worked. So, after that first incident, he started pulling me everywhere—to his room, to the basement, to the front door, to the refrigerator. His glee at his successes was irresistible, so I complied whenever possible.

Then, one day, I saw him reach for Matthew's hand.

"Come on, Matty. Jonny's bed. Play," he said.

Matthew appeared stunned for a moment and he would not take Jonathan's hand. But when his brother repeated his request, Matthew followed. Jonathan decided that was good enough. He dropped his hand to his side and simply led the way. They played for almost an hour, jumping on their beds and crashing back down in unison.

That was the day the dynamic began to change.

In the old days (like about two weeks ago), Matthew and Jonathan would go separate ways when freed from their stroller in large play areas. Jonathan, the social one, would seek out an occasional playmate. Matthew preferred to play on his own. Toward the end, when they both grew tired, they would come together and play. That's how I knew it was almost time to go.

No more.

I first noticed it at the playground last week. After a few minutes of independence, Jonathan sought out Matthew. "Come on, Matty. Come slide," Jonathan said, starting out in the direction of his favorite slide. Without hesitation, Matthew followed. And for the rest of our time there, Jonathan led the way.

The same thing happened at the YMCA toddler pool yesterday.

"Come on, Matty. Jump in water."

"Come on, Matty. Eat Goldfish (the crackers, not the real thing)."

"Come on, Matty. Swim.»

And, again, at the Children's Museum today.

"Come on, Matty. Tunnel."

"Come on, Matty. Roll balls."

"Come on, Matty. Sand."

Where Jonathan went, Matthew followed and he followed willingly.

I'm sure the day will come (soon) when Matthew tires of being the follower and the two struggle over who gets to lead. But that's OK. The point—the thing that makes me so happy inside—is that Matthew and Jonathan find each other to be worthy playmates outside of the home when there are so many other kids to choose from. They are becoming far more than brothers. Like their older brother and sister who are often inseparable, they are becoming friends.

A DIFFERENCE OF WEIGHT

Two years, six months

For the first time ever, Matthew's and Jonathan's weights are significantly different. I first noticed it two weeks ago when they were recovering from colds. Both boys had preferred milk to solids while they were sick, but Matthew tended more toward the liquid diet than Jonathan. So when they stepped on the scale after a bath, I attributed the difference to their illnesses. Matthew weighed in at thirty-three and a half pounds. Jonathan was thirty-five pounds.

But two weeks later, the difference remains.

Part of me wondered whether I was feeding one twin too much or another too little, but then a babysitter put things into perspective: Matthew is much hyper than Jonathan, she noted as she watched them play. And she was right.

Matthew is spontaneous. Always. He moves without thinking and he moves constantly. He rarely stops to eat, though he can't resist a sippy cup full of milk, especially when he is offered his yellow bear and a corner of the sofa with it.

Jonathan, on the other hand, contemplates things more often. He watches his twin brother and he learns from his mistakes. Then he decides whether to act. He does not waste energy. He lets his brother waste it for him. And, boy, does he ever love peanut butter and jelly.

So, it is possible this illness was just the beginning. That Matthew will never make up that caloric difference because he can't be bothered: He is too busy. And that future illnesses will create even greater differences until the two boys are double-digit pounds apart. But then you never know.

Identical twins like to keep parents on their toes.

In utero, Matthew staked out his place as first-born from the beginning (or rather, from the twenty-week ultrasound when we first learned two little guys were hiding out in there). He was head-down right near the cervix when we first saw him and there he stayed. He never gave Jonathan a chance.

Jonathan was all over the place, kicking my ribs, my bladder, and my pelvis. Even after his brother was born, he wouldn't stop moving long enough to come out. He yanked his second foot away every time the doctor tried to breech extract him and took off swimming. When he finally decided to join the world twenty minutes later, he took a spontaneous pike dive, engaging fully head and foot first, and had to be removed via emergency c-section.

The boys were seven ounces apart and Jonathan was the lightweight.

I'm learning that just when I think I understand Matthew and Jonathan, that I know who they are and why they behave like they do, they pull a switch on me. So I'm not going to worry. Instead, I'm going to sit back and enjoy the ride.

SEEING EACH OTHER WITHOUT SEEING DOUBLE

Two years, six months

Matthew and Jonathan have plenty of toys that are duplicates of each other. They have two Thomas the Trains, two Percys, two Gordons, two Lightening McQueens, two school buses, two dump trucks, two ride-on inch worms, two of most any vehicle that they might fight over.

But their white cars are an exception.

Both are white, both are sports cars and they are about the same size, but the two cars are different models. Yet, it was these cars that Matthew pointed to the other day when looked up at me, his eyes bright, and said, "twins!"

Jonathan looked on with interest as Matthew repeated his revelation over and over again.

Then, less than half an hour later, Jonathan pulled out two Diego vehicles. One was a pick-up truck and one was a jeep-like vehicle, but both were yellow and both held figures of Diego and Baby Jaguar snuggled close to one another.

"Twins!" Jonathan said proudly.

Maybe it was just a coincidence. Maybe, at two and a half years old, they don't know what the heck they are talking about. Maybe I over-reacted. But it was one of those identical twins moments that hit me hard, right in the chest, right in the stomach, right in my heart. These two boys who look so much alike, who were born of the same egg and share the same DNA, did not relate their status to that of the replicated vehicles, differentiated only by wear and tear. Instead, they chose vehicles that look similar at first glance, but that are, in reality, unique from each other.

Just like them.

BEWARE THE WAIL OF THE TWIN SIRENS

Two years, seven months

It started as a whimper and it was irresistible.

I can't remember the date, but I do remember that a few weeks ago Jonathan held his arms up to me and whimpered ever so slightly. When I picked him up, he wrapped his toddler fingers around my neck and buried his head in my chest. And I held him there for the longest time, enjoying his warmth, loving that he needed me.

But that whimper became a full-blown wail today.

And it's not so cute anymore.

Jonathan has become my clingy one. His once-adorable whimper now makes my blood pressure rise. His outstretched arms are dangerous. He grabs my legs and trips me. He grabs my arms and spills whatever I am carrying. He grabs my shirt and pulls me backwards, throwing me off balance.

Until today, Matthew has simply looked on.

He has patiently waited for something else to attract Jonathan's attention, knowing that I would give him his share of hugs and cuddles the second my arms were free. Sure. Every now and then, the two of them would start to battle over that space on my lap, but, in the end, Matthew would relent. And he never whimpered.

Until today.

Today was third day of preschool. The twins are attending two mornings a week. They had a blast the first day. Jonathan cried a little when he realized I was leaving, but he couldn't resist the lure of the new toys, the new kids and the novelty of it all. They were tired when I picked them up, but tired in a happy, worn-out kind of way. The second day was much the same. But this morning, Jonathan began to whimper just outside the room. And I could see Matthew perk up.

Matthew was about to go through the classroom doorway when he turned back to me, bright-eyed and determined. He stretched out his arms and began to whimper. Jonathan was stunned for just a second, but then he whimpered louder. And Matthew whimpered louder. And Jonathan cried. And Matthew cried. And Jonathan began to wail.

I couldn't pick them both up while carrying backpacks, so I tried to lead them in by the hands. They threw themselves down on the floor and refused to budge. The teacher came out and grabbed one. The director grabbed the other. I kissed them good-bye and lingered outside the door.

Finally, I asked a passing dad to peek in and give me a report. Each boy was snuggled in a set of arms, he said. They seemed happy, but they were whimpering just a little.

"It was so cute," he said.

And, despite the stress of the morning—despite my throbbing veins, my aching head and my queasy stomach—I was suddenly overwhelmed with a new feeling. One I didn't like because it hurt too much. I was jealous.

I was jealous of the teacher and the director who held Matthew and Jonathan in their arms, feeling those toddler fingers wrap around their necks and those heads buried in their chests. Feeling their warmth. Feeling loved. Feeling needed.

THEY SING!

Two years, seven months

They sing!

Matthew and Jonathan sing!

They sing everything: lullabies; theme songs, "Twinkle, Twinkle;" "I've Been Working on the Railroad," "The Wheels on the Bus." They lie on their beds and sing to Laurie Berkner. They dance in their room and sing with Laurie Berkner. They twist and twirl and flap their hands, and sing with the Wiggles. Their voices are beautiful. Imperfect and beautiful.

They are confident.

They are proud.

They are having a blast.

This, despite the fact that I rarely expose them to raw music.

They get too much TV, too many DVDs.

I did the opposite with my older kids. I was strict with television and I kept the music playing—in the car, in the living room, in their bedrooms. We listened to Laurie Berkner, Raffie, World Playground. I had more energy. Yet my older children rarely belted out tunes at this age. Now, my son sings only in bathrooms and my daughter thinks she's the next Hannah Montana.

But, when I pop in a CD for the twins, they are captivated.

Absolutely.

The best part? Matthew and Jonathan used to say "No sing!" whenever I tried to sing them a lullaby. I can't really blame them. I have this problem with singing on key. But I craved that connection with them, that warm, sweet cuddle time. That has changed. A few months ago, Jonathan crawled into my arms and said, "Rock-a-bye?"

I held him and rocked and sang to him as tears welled in his eyes and trickled down his cheeks. A few days later, Matthew did the same. Now I sometimes rock and sing to both in the recliner or sneak them in another room one-by-one. And each time, they cry. Tears of relief, I think, or of release. And while they let it all go, I take it all in. All of their sweetness.

THE BOOK STORE
Two years, seven months

I have noticed that identical twins often have identical temperaments, or at least they are usually pretty darned close. And that can be a good thing.

Take my friend Misty who has identical triplets. I first met her about four years ago at the YMCA. Her girls were three years old. They lined up to go potty when asked and then they lined up to dress in their swim suits. They walked, not ran, out the door and headed for the pool. I have never seen those girls misbehave. It's just not in their triplet nature.

Matthew and Jonathan are a whole different story. They are highly active, highly curious and stubborn. I have become so accustomed to planning outings in fenced-in areas, running errands at night when my husband is home, and instinctively dreaming up new distractions before the current ones wear off, that I forget just how powerful this combined temperamental force is, and just how often I bow to it. I forget until it hits me head-on, like yesterday.

Over the past few days, I have been trying to plan an afternoon play date with a mom of a three-year-old boy. My first suggestion was a fenced-in playground. I never considered anyplace else. The children's gym that I often rely on closes at 2 p.m. Fortunately, the other mom liked the idea. But then it rained. I was baffled.

These guys refuse to ride in strollers or their wagon. When forced into either one, they take their anger out on each other, kicking and hitting like little mad men. They will hold my hand for short durations, but when it's over, it's over. I've gotten very good at carrying them in a double football hold. In frustration, I once resorted to those harnesses, the cute little puppy ones that look like backpacks. Matthew and Jonathan sat on the concrete as soon as they realized that their freedom was limited and refused to budge.

(Anybody need a couple of barely used harnesses?)

So, on rainy days in the late afternoon when we've already been to the YMCA and the children's gym is closed, we go nowhere. That's home time. Dangerous time. It's the kind of time when toy dolphins swim in toilet water, glass coffee tables become human launching pads and the entire main floor becomes a highly dangerous race track. But I really wanted to meet up with this mom, a fellow writer, so I decided that, for once, I would just have to be brave.

She had suggested Joseph-Beth Booksellers, a large book store in Cincinnati about twenty-five minutes from home. She assured me the book-store had a separate children's area with a train table and a play kitchen, two of the twins' favorite things. So we went. And, to my amazement, we survived.

With their newness, the kitchen and the trains were the main attraction. By the time they'd lost interest, her son was ready to leave to. We walked out of Joseph-Beth holding hands, carrying the price of admission: two stuffed snakes.

It will be quite a while before we can return. After my new friend left, Jonathan found the door and tried to leave. Meanwhile, Matthew had gone back to the snakes and was pulling them off the display one by one. They were getting to comfortable. The newness had worn off.

Still, it was nice.

It was different.

It gave me hope.

Maybe someday I'll even be able to browse the books.

IN SICKNESS OR IN HEALTH
Two years, eight months

It was a terrified cry.

The same kind of cry that had pierced my dreams 26 hours earlier when Matthew vomited in bed while lying on his back. When I found him, it was obvious that Matthew had choked on his vomit and had coughed it out of his throat to get air. So, despite the lack of sleep the night before, I flew out of bed and down the stairs.

What I saw made my heart melt.

Jonathan, who had bemoaned the temporary loss of his playmate all of the previous day, had crawled into Matthew's bed and was snuggling up next to him, scaring him out of a deep sleep. I resettled them both and they quickly fell back asleep.

Jonathan has been feeling Matthew's misery throughout this illness that has lasted forty-eight hours so far and has kept Matthew from venturing more than two feet from the recliner, Matthew and Jonathan are too young to fully understand its meaning. Yet, the depth of their empathy leaves me in awe.

Several times today, Jonathan stopped his play and climbed into the recliner beside his brother, an act that is usually met with kicking hitting and screaming on the occupant's part. But today, Matthew didn't fight it and Jonathan didn't try to kick him out. They sat together for long period of time and watching *Max and Ruby*, *Diego* and *Little Bear*.

Just a few minutes ago, Matthew started to vomit again. I grabbed the bucket and Jonathan grabbed the other side. We held it together while Matthew heaved and heaved until he had nothing left. Then I cleaned Matthew up and sat him in the recliner once again. And Jonathan climbed in beside him.

IDENTICAL TWINS LIVE LONGER

Scientists have good news for identical twins. A 2016 study published in the journal *Plos One* shows identical twins live longer, in general, than people who do not have identical twins. The key, they say, is the intensity of the social and emotional bond between them.

Identical twins tend to protect each other and predict each other's needs better than their singleton counterparts, better even than fraternal twins. That kind of support leads to better health overall and longer lives.

The study is good news for singletons as well. It shows the importance of creating and maintaining strong emotional and social bonds for the sake of our health.

NO MORE PRESCHOOL. THIS IS WHY...
Two years, eight months

I thought I was doing the best thing for all of us when I pulled the twins from the sitter's and sent them to a formal, private preschool two mornings a week (They are still too young for the public preschool.). They loved their sitter and, even while they attended preschool, she still took them one morning a week, but I needed more consistency and I felt they needed more social interaction.

Their sitter is a neighbor's nanny. Whenever the neighbor's children were sick, she had to cancel. Whenever, she was sick, she had to cancel. Whenever our kids were sick, we had to cancel. Then there were vacations to deal with: hers, ours and the parents of the other children. I don't need a lot of time to focus on my writing, run some errands and get a little cleaning done. Nine hours a week is plenty right now, but I really need that nine hours. Even six will do. Heck, when I'm desperate, three is better than nothing.

At the preschool, they would stay home only when they were sick and they had seven other children in their class along with an assistant. The school promised help with potty training, drinking from cups and following directions. It sounded great, it was highly recommended and the twins enjoyed the tour. They were reluctant that first week, but by the second week, they were happy. Sort of. Compliant was more like it.

So I pushed that nagging feeling further back in my mind and labeled it "mommy guilt," guilt over the fact that I had placed my twins in a formal school setting at only two and a half years old, something I never would have considered with my older kids. But an incident today finally opened my eyes.

Matthew had dropped his sippy cup in the parking lot. It slid under a car. He wasn't supposed to bring it into preschool anyway, but, like any toddler, he was devastated by the thought of leaving it there even for a few minutes. While I tried to retrieve it, Jonathan ran into the parking lot. Not good.

So I coaxed them inside with Matthew crying.

I explained the situation to the teacher and tried to tell Matthew I would get it and come right back to show him. He wasn't buying it. The tears flowed harder and that triggered a waterfall from Jonathan. Ten minutes passed and the teacher did nothing to help me. In the end, I had no choice, but to leave with the twins in tow. The teacher smiled and offered words of sympathy, but that was it.

As I buckled Matthew and Jonathan into their car seats with tears flowing down my own cheeks by now, something occurred to me. That teacher did not know these boys as Matthew and Jonathan. She knew them as "The Identical Twins." Just last week, she told me that she couldn't see any differences between them. I took a few minutes to point out physical differences, and then behavioral differences. She shrugged. She just didn't see it.

Now, I don't expect people to be able to apply the differences to the appropriate children, especially if they see them only in a classroom setting twice a week. But I would expect that after a month or so, this woman would at least see that there were differences. She could have if she had tried. But she didn't care to try.

So when I got home, I picked up the phone and I called their sitter.

I apologized for pulling them in the first place and begged her to take them more often. "They slam the door in my face and say 'Bye, mom,' when I leave them with you," I said. "You don't need name tags and you never have. They adore you and I feel like you care for them," I told her.

She didn't even hesitate.

Matthew and Jonathan start their new schedule tomorrow.

RULES OF ENGAGEMENT

Two years, nine months

I've never seen Jonathan quite so stunned. We were at my daughter's tumbling class Monday evening and the twins were playing with a few other toddlers and preschoolers in the observation area. Jonathan wanted a train the other boy was playing with. So he did what he always does. He made an offering, a toy-for-a-toy.

The boy declined again and again and again. Jonathan didn't know what else to do. So he just sat there. He sat there and he stared. Eventually, he found his toy school bus and rejoined Matthew, racing the buses up and down the floor.

You see, Jonathan and Matthew have an understanding. If Jonathan wants Matthew's toy, he keeps offering Matthew something else until Matthew trades. Matthew negotiates in the same way with his twin. It's quite diplomatic... most of the time. But this boy wasn't buying it. He had the favored train and he wasn't about to let go.

This twinese thing isn't just about language. As Jonathan and Matthew grow older, they are developing their own ways of accommodating and playing with each other. They understand each other's intentions with simple nods and gestures. They play games with each other's plates at the dinner table and only they know the rules. They make faces at each other and start laughing, clearly referring back to some event or memory that they share. With one word, one twin engages the other in a preconceived game.

I watch them and I envy them.

I can't imagine what it must be like to know someone so well.

But, at the same time, I fear for them. This bond, the bond that makes them unique, will also hurt them sometimes. At some point, they will have to learn the hard way how to let others in. They won't always be able to ignore the boy with the train and turn to their built-in playmate for social comfort. Sometimes, they will have to learn to pick up another toy and figure out how to play with him. They will not always have each other and it's not healthy for them to know only each other deeply.

So, as they grow, we will have to guide them as best we can without compromising their bond. Their bond has allowed them to skip the stage of parallel play, where toddlers play near each other, observe each other in play, imitate each other and, in doing so, learn social codes of engagement that lead to friendship.

We will have to walk them through it.

Now, if only I knew the way.

IDENTICAL TWINS, IDENTICAL GIFTS?

Two years, eleven months

I am a coward.

I know I should be buying Matthew and Jonathan each drastically different Christmas gifts to help them differentiate from each other, to see themselves as individuals. But it's not going to happen.

Oh, they'll find a few things under the tree that are non-identical. I hit the jackpot with Thomas the Tank Engine characters on EBay and got a whole bunch cheap. So Matthew with get Emily, Dennis, and Bill and Ben. Jonathan will get Rosie, Toby, and Annie and Clarabel.

But they inherited a slew of engines from their older brother last year and they already have doubles of their favorite engines (Thomas, Gordon and Percy). So chances are good that they will simply add these new ones to the bin and happily share them.

Not so with the train T-shirts. (Jonathan chased his brother all over the house yesterday trying to tear off his Power Rangers T-shirt, the only one we have.) Or the doctor kits. (One stethoscope? Are you kidding? Doctors don't have to share. Why should they?) Or the *Cars* helmets. (Different helmets could create a hazardous situation in this household.)

So they will each get a Mader car and a Thomas flashlight and a set of Take-Along tracks. They will both get Thomas place mats and a set of four little cars and the same goodies in their stockings. They will get gifts to share from their siblings and gifts that are just slightly different from an aunt and uncle. We bought them puzzles that are the same size and same difficulty level with closely related themes.

But Matthew and Jonathan are two years old (almost three) and, at this point in their lives, their interests are just about the same. It is not simply because they are identical twins (though I believe that does have something to do with it). It is because they are little and their experiences in life are slim. They love the things that most toddler/preschoolers love. They have always been attracted to similar colors and textures, and it's just not worth the battles right now.

It wasn't worth it with our older kids, who are seventeen months apart, either.

Over the next year, Jonathan and Matthew will start to develop more as individuals. They will experience things differently more often. They will start to cultivate their own interests. We will help them do that by exposing them to as much as we can and encouraging them each to explore those concepts and activities that attract them most.

But right now, I just want them to be happy.

And, to be honest, I want to have a peaceful Christmas.

So, a coward I am.

OUR BOYS
THAT ONE

Two years, eleven months

The realization hit me just before Christmas.

It was early in the evening and all four kids were playing together. My daughter stopped to describe a funny incident involving one of her twin brothers. I asked her which one. She pointed to Matthew and said, "That one."

"Who?" I asked.

"That one," she said.

"No," I said. "Tell me his name."

She shrugged and said she didn't know. Then I asked her older brother. He didn't know either. Neither was bothered. Matthew and Jonathan were indistinguishable to even their own siblings. How could we have missed that? We missed it because we were too busy.

When all four children are together, the household is a chaotic mess. They twins like to get wild and the older kids like to get wild with them. It's all I can do to keep my sanity and to ensure that no one gets hurt. Who has time for individuality and identities?

I didn't let it go that evening. I pressed my older children to figure out who was who and, in the end, they got it right. When we sat down to breakfast the next morning, we had a chat. Riley (nine) and Kiersten (eight) told me that they can figure out who is who if they really try, but that they usually didn't bother. They didn't bother, they said, because I was always quick to identify their brothers for them.

We reached an agreement. I explained why it was important that they know their brothers as individuals. They agreed to try. For a day or two, it was a game. It quickly became a habit. There are still times when they refer to the twins as "this one," or "that one," but most of the time it's "Matt," or "Jon."

And something beautiful has come of it. Their strategy of play has changed. Riley and Kiersten are learning that Matthew and Jonathan have different play styles and that simply getting wild isn't the only option. Riley and Jonathan have a cuddling game. Kiersten enjoys engaging Matthew in conversation.

The house is quieter (sometimes).

The kids are more content (sometimes).

I am much less stressed.

PART 3

The Preschool Years

(Ages 3 to 5 years)

The preschool years are marked by uninhibited creativity and curiosity. The joy and wonderment of this period is unmatched by any other. Witnessing this kind of growth through one child is magical, but the rewards are more than doubled with identical twins. We get to experience their growth as individuals, but we also get to observe as their relationships with each other evolve. Each twin will develop his own way of relating to the world, but each will do so with the support of the other. They will come together. They will pull apart. They will test the boundaries of their bonds just as they test all other limits in life. The preschool years are a period of twin development that can only be described as awesome.

TODAY THEY ARE THREE

Three years

My first thought on the twins' second birthday was, "Thank God. They are halfway to four." I make no apologies. Those were tough days. But today, they are three. Today is different. Today, I am excited.

These two little men can talk to me. They can reason with me. They can argue with me. They can sympathize. They can empathize. They can stomp their feet. They can hold my hands. They can play hide-n-seek. They can dress themselves. They can leap onto my lap and wrap their arms around my neck for no reason at all. They can tell me stories.

Yes, it's still hard. They still run away from me at times. They still open the fridge, strip off their clothes and sneak into my office to play on my computer. They jump off everything, throw their toys and dump their stuffed-animal basket.

They are demanding, stubborn and curious.

But, they bring their plates to the counter after dinner. They hug and kiss each other when they apologize. They pretend to be their older brother and sister and they pretend to be each other. Their cars and trains go grocery shopping, to school and to Target. The best part is that they do most of that in different ways.

Matthew is Matthew.

Jonathan is Jonathan.

They are inseparable, but separate.

I let them choose the flavor ice-cream they will have with their cakes today. Matthew chose chocolate. Jonathan chose vanilla. Each will savor his own, but each will try the other's. Today, they are three. And, this time around, I feel no urge to rush it. I look forward to the journey that will take us to four.

THE GAMES THEY PLAY

Three years, one month

The rice was cooking. The ground turkey was soaking up the taco spices. The black beans (protein for our vegetarian son) were in the microwave. Dinner was almost ready the other day when my domestic bliss was disturbed by a frantic, high-pitched cry.

"Help! Help! Someone help me!"

I darted into the living room, afraid of the scene that might await me. What I found made my heart stop... in a good way. Jonathan stood on the edge of the sofa in a crouch. Matthew stood below him with his arms outstretched.

"I will help you, Jonny," Matthew said in a soft voice. "I will help you."

Jonathan leaped gently into his brother's arms and both boys crashed to the floor in a fit of giggles. Then Matthew climbed onto the sofa, stood in a crouch on the edge and yelled, "Help! Help!" while Jonathan reached out to him.

It was a game. Just a game. New, complicated, highly imaginative games are becoming an important part of Matthew's and Jonathan's twin life lately. Among their favorites: They serve each other pizza and salads; they use a toy blood-pressure monitor as a racing flag and take turns running to an imaginary finish line; they have rules about who can shout "bah" and when while they are watching DVDs.

Even more interesting is that they are in agreement.

Matthew and Jonathan do not argue about the rules. When one chastises the other for breaking a rule, the scolded twin complies. Neither tries to take control over the other. They don't question each other's judgment.

Oh, I'm sure their time will come. They are only three, after all. But I am living in the moment and right now, I am in awe of them. I am loving it.

THE TIME-OUT SWAP

Three years, one month

I used to be able to count on Matthew to keep me on track or, at least count on his time-outs. He'd begin testing me immediately after we dropped the older kids off at school. By the second trip to the time-out chair, I knew, without looking at the clock, that it was time to get lunch ready.

The third trip generally came just before we left to pick up the older kids from school, and fourth time-out was our call to dinner. Sometimes, there was a fifth time-out. That meant we were late getting them to bed. But I couldn't count on Jonathan. Just the mention of discipline made him quiver. And whenever his brother was placed in the time-out chair, he would cry and cry, demanding that I set him free. I could honestly say that Matthew was our difficult twin.

Not anymore.

Just as they have done with so many other personality traits, Matthew and Jonathan have swapped. It's almost like they are toying with us. They push us and push us to label them, and then, just when we're confident that we know these guys, that we know who they are and that we can openly say so, they pull a fast one.

One takes on the trait of the other.

But that doesn't mean they mimic each other. Somehow, they still manage to do it in their own, individual ways. Yes, Matthew's behavior has improved. But he doesn't have the empathy that Jonathan had. He couldn't care less whether his brother gets a time-out.

And I can't count on Jonathan like I could count on Matthew. Jonathan's time-outs come in one endless stream all day long and they are proceeded by screeches of "I don't like," I don't," and "I will not" along with lots of hitting and pushing. Matthew simply defied us, quietly and boldly.

I'm not thrilled with this phase, but I am thrilled to find even more evidence that identical genes do not mean that Matthew and Jonathan will respond to situations with identical emotions and attitudes. Even in their rebellion, they are individuals.

FREAKS, WEIRDOS, SLAP-STICK DUOS: IDENTICAL TWINS ON TELEVISION

Three years, two months

After a long, hard swimming lesson today, Matthew and Jonathan kicked back on the sofa with a couple sippies of milk (white for Jonathan; chocolate for Matthew) and tuned into an episode of *Olivia*, the animated series about an imaginative girl pig who is obsessed with red.

I didn't catch all of it, but I found myself pulled in when Olivia introduced a set of identical twin pigs, who were boys. She mixed up their names, of course, and they pointed out her error. Olivia's response? She laughed and referred to them instead as, simply "twins."

The identical boys then performed the equivalent of a circus act.

This from Nick Jr., the network that proclaims to defy stereotypes and introduce children to a diversity of peoples and cultures with such shows as *Dora the Explorer* and *Ni Hao Kia-Lan*. I have always been annoyed by the portrayal of identical twins in film and in television. When they are the main characters, they sometimes fare well. But when they are secondary characters, they are most often the slapstick duos, the weirdoes, the freaks.

They are not hard to find, particularly in the popular animated televisions series targeted at children—the Egg twins (Eggbert and Leo) in *Oswald*; Timmy and Tommy Tibble in *Arthur*; Susan and Mary Test from *Johnny Test*—just to name a few.

Now that we are raising identical twins of our own, I am more than annoyed. I am concerned for my youngest sons and the message these portrayals relay to them. These shows treat identical twins as hilarious units, as misfits, as circus acts.

And as I look at our boys sitting there on the sofa—one in shorts, the other in pants; one in a red shirt, the other in yellow; both with their heads cocked in precisely the same position with precisely the same expression on their handsome faces—I can't help thinking that this is hard enough.

Already, their strikingly similar looks and mannerisms require they announce their individual identities daily, something other children never have to worry about. But now they have to fight Nick Jr. too, and PBS and Disney and all the authors out there who use identical twins as devices.

The worst part?

(Maybe I'm overreacting. Maybe they'll never put two and two together. They are smart boys, smart enough to avoid identifying with cartoon characters. Smart enough to differentiate fiction from reality even at three years old. Maybe, I've just had too long a day and this rant is just the result of stress.) When the identical boys on *Olivia* performed their clownish act, Matthew and Jonathan laughed.

POTTY TRAINING: A DIVISION OF LABOR

Three years, two months

Tomorrow is a big day for Matthew. Tomorrow he will wear underwear all day long for the first time and Jonathan will not. Matthew has been using the potty for months now. Until recently, he was inconsistent. He would pee on the potty or toilet when we set him there, but he would not ask to go and he would fight the suggestion. And number two? No way. He wouldn't even consider it. But something clicked a few weeks ago and, much to our relief, he's ready.

Matthew is about to graduate from toddler to "big boy," but he's leaving his twin brother behind. Far behind. And, for once, we're not worried. If they follow their usual pattern, Jonathan will be whizzing like a pro in no time.

Jonathan has taken this same approach to each milestone since birth. Over the past three years, he has sat idly by while his brother struggled to roll over, sit up, crawl, stand and walk. And Matthew worked so hard.

He plugged away, sometimes for months at a time, until, finally, the day of celebration arrived.

In the beginning, it worried me.

Who am I kidding? It terrified me.

I remember clearly one telephone conversation in the spring of 2007.

"Jonathan won't roll over," I told the pediatrician, nearly in tears. "His brother worked on it for months and is rolling well, but Jonny just lies there and watches him. He doesn't make any effort at all. He doesn't even rock on his side."

"Well, maybe it would be a good idea to have him evaluated," the doctor said in that I'm-not-trying-to-worry-you-but-this-could-be-serious kind of voice (a tone of voice that, in my stressed-out state, I probably imagined). "He really should at least be interested in rolling by now. I can refer you to an excellent therapist."

I hung up the phone with every intention of dialing again and making that appointment. But I got distracted. I don't remember what happened—whether it was a diaper change, a feeding, Matthew rolling out of the safety zone—but, for whatever reason, I postponed that phone call. Within hours, Jonathan started rolling. There was no struggle. He just rolled and he rolled well. He rolled with more ease and more speed than Matthew.

And that's the way it went from then on.

For each milestone, Jonathan waited until Matthew achieved perfection and then he immediately surpassed him. And he's doing it again, we hope. Jonathan has been Matthew's greatest potty-training supporter. He follows him into the bathroom. He flushes the toilet for him. He does the "yippee" dance whenever Matthew succeeds, sincerely thrilled for his twin brother. But when we ask him whether he wants to try, his answer is firm: "No."

Bribes, charts and positive reinforcement are useless. He is immune to them. We leave the bathroom defeated and deflated and, if we've annoyed Jonathan enough, sometimes even bruised. We know better, or at least we should.

We should know that Jonathan will wait until Matthew is comfortable in his underwear and accident-free. He will wait until all the mistakes have been made and corrected. He will wait until the process is ingrained in his being, until every movement, every bit of required coordination that he witnessed over these past several month, is part of his own psyche, his own experience.

Then Jonathan will approach that toilet and he will attempt to one-up his twin brother.

He won't bother sitting on the seat.

He will pee standing up.

AGGRESSIVE AFFECTION

Three years, three months

I've come up with a new term to describe the way Matthew and Jonathan relate to each other. I've decided to call it "aggressive affection."

It starts off sweet. One grabs the other around the waist or shoulders, leans his head against his twin, grins and makes baby noises. Most often, the other responds in kind. It's a Hallmark moment, or a Kodak moment, or something like that.

Until it's not.

Usually, within about five minutes, hugging becomes flinging. Flinging becomes wrestling. Grins turn to giggles. Wrestling results in head stomping, eye poking or chest crushing. Giggles evolve into tears. I should probably stop it before it even begins, but I can't. When I watch them standing there with their arms around each other, their heads together and those untamed smiles on their faces, I am reminded of their infancy. I remember when we would put them down at night crossways on opposite sides of their crib only to find them together in the middle minutes later with their heads touching.

Sometimes, we'd find them holding hands.

They don't intend to hurt each other during their wrestling matches. They just get carried away. I like to think that they get too aggressive simply because of their need to be physically close to each. Hence, the justification for my new term for their sometimes bloody battles (Matthew's head whacked Jonathan's face a few days ago, leaving Jonathan with a bloody nose. A few days before that, Jonathan re-opened a small cut on Matthew's leg.): Aggressive affection. Sweet, huh?

A CASE OF MISTAKEN IDENTITY

Three years, four months

I often tell people that, these days, I find it hard to believe Matthew and Jonathan are identical. I know we have the DNA tests to prove it, but I look at them and I see so very many differences that I wonder how anyone could mix them up at all. Then comes a day like today.

The boys were playing with trains and cars. Matthew had been racing with Lightning McQueen in a toy garage for at least half an hour while Jonathan had been more interested in the trains. The boys decided they needed tracks of both kinds, so we dumped a few bins and started to build. One twin focused on creating a large and winding train track while the other worked on city streets. Then they picked up vehicles and started to play.

In less than a minute, a full-fledged brawl had broken out.

Jonathan kept trying to take Lightning from Matthew, who had been building the city. I tried offering him one of the five other Lightning McQueens they own (Yes, they are obsessed!), but he refused, insisting that particular car was his and fighting to get it back. So I disciplined Jonathan with a time out.

Or so I thought.

Jonathan's wail as he sat in that chair was one of absolute despair. That was odd. Jonathan usually rages with anger in the time-out chair. I looked more closely and saw the tiny red spider vein by the right eye. It was Matthew. No wonder he had expressed such despair: it really was his car. The other twin should have been in the time-out chair.

I pulled Matthew up into my arms, held him tight and apologized over and over and over again. I carried him to where Jonathan was playing and offered him another Lightning car in exchange. Jonathan readily agreed and the two brothers played together on the city streets that Jonathan, not Matthew, had built.

It seems Matthew has forgiven me. I hope he has more of that forgiveness within him and that Jonathan has a wealth of it too because I am beginning to realize that I will need it. I will need lots of it and so will the many other people in their lives. And I promise that I will never doubt their zygosity again. They are, indeed, identical twins.

IDENTICAL TWINS HAVE DIFFERENT FINGERPRINTS

Sorry, identical twins. You cannot leave fingerprints at a crime scene and try to pin the crime on your twin. Identical twins have very similar fingerprints, but they are not entirely the same. Their prints have high correlations of loops, whorls and ridges, but the details—such as where skin ridges meet, divide into branches, or end—differ, according to the Washington State Twin Registry.

The organization, which tracks identical twins over time for a variety of studies, explains it this way: Fingerprints are determined by the interaction of genes in the developmental environment of the womb. Their patterns are set between the thirteenth and nineteenth weeks of development and are influenced by a variety of environmental factors. Examples include differences in umbilical cord length (which can influence blood flow), access to nutrition, blood pressure, rate of finger growth at the end of the first trimester, and position in the womb.

THE POTTY THAT DIVIDES THEM

Three years, four months

Jonathan has thrown me for a loop. It's been two months since Matthew became a "big boy" and started wearing underwear and Jonathan still wants nothing to do with the potty. Nothing. I persuaded him to pee on the potty once, but only through trickery and he's not about to fall for that again.

Jonathan is breaking the pattern he and Matthew have followed since birth. He had always allowed Matthew to perfect the major physical milestones and then, just as we admitted the need for professional intervention, he achieved the milestone and surpassed his twin within days.

Not this time.

If we even suggest that he pee in his little Bjorn potty, or on the toilet, or while sitting on the ring on the toilet, or while standing in the bathroom next to the toilet, or in any darned way he pleases, he clenches his fists with his arms at his sides, adopts a deep voice and growls, "no." I am perplexed. We have tried pushing him, bribing him, letting him be. Nothing works.

Jonathan has sought out every other way in which to express his maturity. While Matthew is comfortable in his three-year-old skin, Jonathan is eight years old most days. Some days he declares he's nine. Today he was ten, like his big brother Riley, he said. He said he was eighteen last week because he wanted to be old enough to drive a bus.

He screams, hollers and take the spatula out of my hands when I cook because he wants to do it too. He takes the grapes from the refrigerator, carries them to the table and plucks off his own. He puts them back. He was furious the other day because he wanted to start the car and I wouldn't let him.

He puts on his own shoes now. He opens all doors by himself. He pushes a chair up to the counter when the phone rings and tries to answer it before I can. He wipes tables with sponges. He cleans melted Popsicle from the floor with paper towel. He brushes his own teeth morning and night and fights me bitterly when I insist on a turn. But he will not pee on the potty. I am defeated, deflated, discouraged.

I think.

There is one possibility, one hope that I cling to. It occurred to me this afternoon as I tossed Matthew's moist underwear and shorts down the laundry shoot. Matthew still has accidents. He's getting better and some days he has none. But on most days, especially near bedtime, we can count on either a trickle or a puddle. Matthew grows too tired or too distracted to get to the bathroom on time and, at that hour, Jonathan is rarely far away.

He sees it.

Matthew is potty trained in our eyes, but maybe not in Jonathan's. Maybe Jonathan is still waiting for perfection. Maybe Jonathan will not put his pee where it belongs until Matthew has made it through a few days in a row accident free. Jonathan is a demanding little guy. And he can be awfully hard on his identical twin. Perhaps the pattern isn't really broken. Maybe we're just looking at it from the wrong perspective. I hope.

IDENTICAL TWINS, IDENTICAL CLASSROOM: WHY THEY WILL STUDY TOGETHER

Three years, six months

It's starting already. Family members, friends, even strangers in malls and grocery stores. They mean well. I really think they do, but they are ill-informed through no fault of their own. The lead-in could easily be mistaken for the question.

"Are you planning to send the twins to preschool?" they ask.

Then comes the question, which isn't really a question at all.

"You will separate them, right?"

Followed by the silence when I answer, with confidence.

"No."

But, like I said, the attitude isn't really their fault.

For the past few decades, the prevalent theory among educators has been that all twins fare better when separated in school. It helps them develop individual identities, they say, particularly with identical twins. It gives them more confidence, they argue. It helps them make friends of their own. But here's the trouble: no evidence exists to support those recommendations, policies or decisions.

Quite the opposite, in fact.

The few studies done on the effects of separating twins in elementary school show that most twins suffer emotionally and socially, and that for identical twins, separation can be highly traumatic and might impact academic performance as well. Consider this finding from a 2004 study conducted by the Institute of Psychiatry at Kings College in London:

"When compared to those not separated, those separated early had significantly more teacher-rated internalizing problems and those separated later showed more internalizing problems and lower reading scores. Monozygotic (MZ) twins showed more problems as a result of separation than dizygotic (DZ) twins."

Or this finding from a 2010 University of Amsterdam study of 1,839 monozygotic and 1,164 dizygotic twin pairs: (This study focused primarily on the effects on academic performance.)

"There is no difference in educational achievement between twins who share a classroom and twins who do not share a classroom during their primary school time. The choice of separation should be made by teachers, parents and their twin children, based on individual characteristics of a twin pair."

The same folks who believe Matthew and Jonathan should each strike out on their own by age three wouldn't hesitate to put their own children in classrooms with their best friends. After all, that kind of kinship puts children at ease, makes them less clingy and allows them to be more socially confident. So why would we separate Matthew or Jonathan from his best friend during this time of stress, excitement and change?

I was relieved today to chat with one of their future preschool teachers, a mother of seventeen-year-old identical twin boys. She kept her boys together throughout the younger years and, as they got older, took them aside separately to ask whether they wanted to stay together the following year, she said. Each year, the answer was the same: yes.

As we spoke about our children, children filtered into the classroom where Matthew and Jonathan were playing. Jonathan immediately befriended two boys his age who took an interest in the same tractor that had attracted him. Matthew squatted near a child-sized sofa conversing with a slightly older girl who had sat down with a book. A barrier of shelves separated Matthew and Jonathan.

Neither panicked at the absence of the other.

Neither looked for the other.

Both put up a good battle when it was time to leave.

And I couldn't help smiling when both boys demanded to know when they could come back.

BRING ON THE BOOKS, FINALLY!

Three years, seven months

We started reading to our older children regularly while they were still young enough to slobber all over the board-book pages. We were determined to instill in them a love of reading and it worked.

Both older kids are avid readers and reading helps keep us close to each of them. At ages ten and almost nine, they still insist that we each snuggle with them in their beds at night and read aloud. When we leave their rooms, they read on their own, often falling asleep with books clenched in their hands or draped over their faces or chests. It didn't work out that way with Matthew and Jonathan and, until recently, I felt we had failed them in that regard.

From birth, Jonathan and Matthew were both highly active and addicted to motion. Books were for throwing and chewing. Lap time was for bouncing and rocking. They were not attracted to pages decorated with bright images or fuzzy rabbit fur or flaps that flipped to reveal surprises.

Add to their physical intensity the stress of raising two older children, one with issues that required a great deal of our emotional and physical attention, and I found that my efforts to intrigue them with books were slipping. It became easier and easier to say, "I'll read to them tomorrow." And too often I made the same promise to myself the next day.

Over time, we learned they would pay attention to books that they could act out with us dramatically and loudly. If we could howl, stomp, clap, yelp, jump or twist and shout, they were happy. So that's what we did. It was fun. Lots of fun. But exhausting. We still read only every other day or so and rarely before bed. Nighttime reading got them too excited and left us drained, but then I discovered Thomas board books.

That was our breakthrough.

Jonathan and Matthew are devout fans of *Thomas the Tank Engine*, so when I found a few books at the grocery store about a year ago, they couldn't get enough of them. Over and over, we read about Thomas and the judge who lost her hat, about the crack in the track, about the race with Bertie the Bus. Little by little, we added non-train books to their reading list until they were finally taking in many of the same classics that our older children had loved.

It was wonderful except for a couple of things: Matthew and Jonathan had to be in precisely the right mood; we had to read to them separately to avoid physically dangerous book wars; and they had no desire to read at bedtime.

Good enough, I figured. Some kids just aren't that into it and that was something I would have to accept. But then something happened just a few short weeks ago. I was unpacking boxes from our recent move and looking for something different to read when I stumbled across *Caps for Sale* by Esphyr Slobodkina. It was too long for them, I figured, and the pictures were not likely to capture their attention, but it was worth a shot.

I was stunned.

We read it nine times that day without a single argument.

So I reached into the bin and pulled out a few more books that I had categorized as above their interest level and, to my surprise, they listened. They listened eagerly, intently and without argument. They begged me to read those same books over and over again. And they sifted through the books themselves, finding even more that captured their interest.

They evolved into different children.

On the same day, at the same time, with the same book as their trigger.

The same boys who once simultaneously shredded two copies of *Mr. Brown Can Moo* now follow us around with books begging for reading time. They grab books and lie on the floor with them pretending to read as they flip through the pages. They fall asleep with books in their hands, books that they have strained to "read" by their night light.

And the best part?

They no longer argue when they sit together on my lap for a story.

They seem to have declared a truce.

A truce because they are finally in love with reading.

WHEN DRESSING IDENTICAL TWINS ALIKE IS A BAD IDEA

Three years, seven months

I have to laugh when people ask whether we ever dress Matthew and Jonathan alike.

As babies, they peed and pooped through so many clothes that we'd have needed at least four sets of all outfits to keep them in matching clothes for more than an hour or two. Identical outfits were not practical anyway, especially in the winter when socks covered Jonathan's painted toenails. It was hard enough to tell them apart. Why would we want to make it harder?

By the time the boys were sixteen months old, they had distinct color preferences and they had learned to exert those preferences loudly and strongly. Matthew wore yellow. Jonathan wore orange. Matthew wore pants. Jonathan wore shorts. Efforts to dress them in matching clothes were met with fury.

Now, at three and a half years old, the boys share few clothes. For the most part, they have each claimed certain shirts, pants, shorts, socks and jackets. On occasion, they will wear the same jackets or the same color shirt, but that's where it ends.

For the most part, it matters not to me whether others dress their identical twins alike. It's fairly harmless when they are young and most kids will protest if they don't like it as they age. By the teen years, many identical twins choose to dress alike anyway. But there are times, I have learned, when dressing identical twins in identical clothing is simply a bad idea.

In public places: I once bought matching swim trunks for Matthew and Jonathan and took them to the toddler pool at the YMCA. What a nightmare. Though the pool is small and a lifeguard is always on duty, it would have been easy for active children like my own to walk out the gate with another family. From even a short distance, it was impossible to tell the boys apart with their naked chests and matching trunks. I was always on edge, making sure I could see both at the same time. It must have been at least as difficult for the lifeguard. How would I know whether one had left and I'd simply seen the other one twice?

I had the same experience at a playground once when they wore matching tops. Though their shorts were different, they were close in color. Someone could easily have snatched one up, or one twin could have run off to the parking lot, and it would have taken me too much precious time to notice that I was not seeing both twins, but rather one twin twice.

At pools, on playgrounds and in public spaces, it can be dangerous to dress twins alike.

When you don't want attention: All infant twins will be ogled. That is a fact parents must accept. They are just far too adorable to resist when they are together in their strollers with their soft skin, tiny cries and pink cheeks. It's best to accept it and build ogle time into our schedules.

Once twins ditch the strollers though, ogling-related disruptions should be greatly reduced. Jonathan and Matthew are always taking off in different directions. Unless they are standing together, it can be difficult to tell whether they are even brothers, so much for twins.

Yet I see it, hear it and read it all the time: moms of toddlers and older twins complaining that they were "stopped once again" by curious strangers in malls, grocery stores and restaurants. They curse the strangers and expound upon the "rudeness" of some people. Just about every time, however, further questioning reveals the twins were dressed alike. The only reason to dress identical twins alike is for the attention. If parents do not want the attention, they should not dress their twins alike.

It's that simple.

When the twins say "No:" This should be a no-brainer.

Our boys surprise me at every turn. So it's possible that despite their firm convictions about clothing, they will someday beg me for matching jeans, t-shirts and sneakers as we are shopping. If they do, I will relent because it really should be up to them from now on, except in those situations where it might be dangerous. I might even think it's cute.

I do not judge those who dress their twins alike. It can be fun. But I must admit I do judge those who do not use common sense. So please, when you dress your identical twins, just use common sense, and then, when you are out and about and I see them pass by in matching outfits, I will be among those who grin and comment on how adorable they are. I might even stop you for a peek at them because twins do that to people. And making people smile, making them happy, is a good thing.

IDENTICAL AWAKENINGS: SHARED DNA AT WORK?

Three years, nine months

I've always believed that shared DNA would have little or no influence on whether Matthew and Jonathan slept through the night. Overall, yes, it would make sense that biology would dictate how much sleep they need and about when they might tire. But disruptions in sleep patterns are most often caused by dreams, right? Experience influences dreams and shared DNA does not always equal shared experiences.

Matthew and Jonathan are often together, but the slightest distractions—from physical positioning to hunger to whether they might have to pee at the time—can shape experiences differently for each child. They take in different things depending on how closely they are paying attention, which senses they are using and the perspective from which they see things. Jonathan and Matthew have had three and a half years' worth of differentiation. That seems like a lot, but something happened last night that made me question my theory, and it's not the first time.

Matthew woke up at about 3 a.m. He wasn't upset or worried. He was just awake. He used the bathroom and I took him back to bed, where we curled up together for about 45 minutes. Finally, I tip-toed out of his room, believing he was asleep.

About an hour later, I spied a young figure at the foot of our bed. I pulled him into bed with me, believing it was Matthew again. He'd awoken the same way: no crying, no worries, just awake. I was tired and he just wasn't crashing, so after a few minutes, my husband took him back to his room, where he realized Matthew's bed was occupied. This was Jonathan.

About 45 minutes after he awoke, Jonathan was again asleep.

Just like Matthew.

Matthew and Jonathan are good sleepers. They always have been. They go down hard and they wake up early, but they sleep like rocks through the night. The few times they have awoken, however, (aside from those moments when they've wet their beds), their awakenings have been so similar in nature that I've found it almost eerie.

If one awakens with a particular cry, the other will awaken with that exact same cry an hour so later—close enough to his twin that we can compare the awakenings, but far enough apart that we can be sure one did not awaken the other.

If one awakens with no cry, the other will soon awaken the same way. And it seems that it takes about the same time and effort to get him back to sleep. Looking back, I don't recall that they have ever awakened differently unless one was sick or had the wet his bed.

I've tried to attribute these common awakenings to coincidence. Maybe one twin tossed and turned in his sleep, triggering frightening dreams in the other. Maybe one twin's awakening caused the other's. But their awakenings are too far apart to persuade me and it's happened far too many times.

I don't believe this is evidence of some kind of twin telepathy, but I have come to believe that brain chemistry strongly influences sleep patterns, especially in children. When our older kids woke up at odd hours, I initially attributed it to stress, bad dreams or other external influences. But in retrospect, it seems there was almost always a biological cause. As a toddler, our oldest son suffered night terrors, which are caused by mini seizures. I don't recall him waking up during the night much after those passed.

Our daughter had nightmares several times a night until she was diagnosed with anxiety, which doctors believe is caused by a chemical imbalance common in people of her intelligence. Once she was treated with medication that stabilized those chemicals, she slept beautifully and still does.

As adults, we often have trouble sleeping because of external stresses. We're thinking about work, relationships, money, all kinds of things as we struggle to sleep, and we often have trouble shutting out those thoughts. All that stress prevents us from producing the hormones and chemicals that override our worries and help us crash for the night.

At three years old, Jonathan and Matthew don't have many of those external worries. And even if they did, what are the chances that their stresses are similar enough to cause them to awaken the same way on the same nights? No, I have to believe that it's their shared DNA that is behind their awakenings. Some sort of chemical change in brain pattern is occurring almost simultaneously. And that makes me wonder about the way we approach childhood sleep disruptions as a society.

Perhaps too often biology is overlooked.

So often, I hear parents say that their children need to "get over it" when they frequently awaken during the night. They take the tough-love approach, simply sending them back to bed in hopes that they will get through this phase if no one pays them heed. Matthew and Jonathan do not have sleep issues. They rarely awaken, but the pattern I have observed when they do wake up during the night is strong evidence that some kids, perhaps many kids, can't help themselves. Maybe some children need more than tough-love.

Maybe, more often than not, the awakenings that parents attribute to bad dreams, clinginess or a need for attention are really biology at work.

FOUR IS ENOUGH

Three years, nine months

I was unloading groceries from the van yesterday when I spied a couple at a neighbor's BBQ with infant twins. They waved. I waved. We started talking, so I crossed the street to take a peek. They were identical boys. Seven weeks old. I waited. And waited. And waited. But the pang never came.

The pang that alluded me had come frequently and unsolicited as our older two children started growing up. It would start to form when I would see a mom with an infant. The "ooo"s and "awe"s would slip from my throat as I remembered how soft and delicate my children were at that age. How innocent and unaffected they were by the greater world. How they fit so perfectly in the cradle of my arm.

Not so since the twins were born.

These babies were adorable, so that wasn't the issue. They were even identical, just like my boys. They were clean and sweet and sleeping peacefully. Still, no pang. Matthew and Jonathan have wiped the pang right out of me. And I don't think that's a bad thing.

I adore my boys just as much as I adore my other two children. I savored and continue to savor each stage of their development, just as I do with the other two. But there is not a single part of me that would want to go through infancy or toddlerhood with highly active, strong, curious, creative identical twin boys ever again. Not even with a singleton. I can't even conjure up a daydream.

So when I looked at those boys, I struggled.

The "ooo"s and "awe"s that parents come to expect just weren't there, and all hope of ever recapturing them was dashed when I learned that the couple had two older children. Instead, I was flooded with memories of fear. Fear that I would not have enough love or attention for four children, especially when two were infants. Unfounded fears.

Definitely unfounded.

The words that came out of my mouth instead were words of encouragement, which led to questions from the parents, which led to more words of encouragement. When the natural time came to end the conversation and go our separate ways, I wasn't sure what to expect. So I was surprised when they said, "Thank you."

"It's so nice," the mom said, "to finally meet someone who understands."

And for me, it was so nice to be understood.

IDENTICAL TWINS BEHAVE IDENTICALLY IN GROUPS, A NEW STUDY SAYS

Three years, ten months

As Jonathan and Matthew grow into adulthood, they are likely to use the same set of moral and ethical guidelines to choose their friends and select the groups they join. They will also be equally stubborn when they have to decide whether to comprise their values when it comes to new group memberships.

The same is not true of fraternal twins.

This is according to a new study by researchers at the University of Edinburgh, published in the November, 2010, issue of the journal, *Psychological Science.* The Edinburgh researchers assessed one thousand pairs of adult twins, both identical and fraternal, to determine whether genetics plays a role in loyalty toward social groups and in how flexible people can be in adapting to group memberships.

The overwhelming finding was that it does affect both membership and flexibility.

Identical twins, who share DNA, functioned equally well or equally poorly in groups, and used the same ethical, religious and racial criteria to make their decisions. The same was not evident of fraternal twins, no matter how well-bonded they were.

Analysts seem to think the study will have military uses.

I agree.

Already, I see that Matthew and Jonathan concur that Batman has a dark side and that the Teenage Mutant Ninja Turtles are cool. They also seem to be equally stubborn about which toys are worth fighting over and they both like preschool. Surely the military can do something with that.

RENDEZVOUS WITH THE GUY IN RED

Three years, eleven months

Both Matthew and Jonathan are fascinated with Santa. They see him every chance they get and they have no fear. None whatsoever. And they leave poor Santa with no time for "Ho, ho, ho" or "Merry Christmas." The cheery old guy is immediately bombarded with questions: "Is that your belt? Is it black? Is it magic? Are those your boots? Can I wear them? Why do you wear gloves? Are they white?"

Santa's appearance at preschool tonight gave the boys one more opportunity.

Matthew immediately headed for the costume rack and dressed up for Santa Claus with a suit vest, a suit coat and a beaded necklace. Jonathan played it cool with his animal tracks T-shirt. Both were equally persistent, however, when he asked what they wanted for Christmas.

"That bag," they said almost simultaneously, pointing to gift bags beside his chair.

Then a pause.

Then, "pleeeaaase!"

NEVER SAY NEVER: TWINS AND HARNESSES

Three years, eleven months

The question I am asked most frequently by parents of younger twins and that I see most often on online forums involves harnesses or leashes. Parents want to know whether I used them with my guys and, if I did, whether they worked.

Before Jonathan and Matthew walked, I will admit, I would have been mortified by the thought. My older kids are seventeen months apart. I taught them to stay with me by gradually allowing them more and more freedom from the stroller and returning them to the stroller when they misbehaved. And it worked beautifully. If it worked for me, it should work for everyone.

Right?

But my older kids have inherently different personalities. My oldest son is quiet, introspective and studious. Rules are meant to be followed and he won't even let me break them. My daughter is fiery, but she is a perfectionist. She rarely ventured from me as a toddler because she wasn't supposed to, and that trait made disobedience disagreeable for her.

The older kids could play together with Play-Doh or Legos or Polly Pockets for hours at a time. They were easily entertained by activities that were mental, or by games that were intricately involved. They loved long hikes, but never really took to baseball or soccer or other competitive sports.

I had no idea how easy I had it.

The twins come from a whole different set of our genes. Like their older siblings, they are intelligent. But they were born to flex their muscles and that need overrules everything else. Bugs are for squishing, not studying. Crayons are for floors and walls, not paper. Imaginative games involve bad guys, running, chasing and wrestling rather than hours constructing cities, amusement parks and other worlds.

They never attempted to earn freedom. They simply took it.

By age two, they were strong enough (They are very strong) and tall enough (They are very tall) to flip themselves over the sides of their stroller with the harnesses still on. I'd turn around to see them dangling from the sides, twisted in the straps. Very dangerous.

No wagon was big enough to prevent them from kicking each other hard in the stomach and face every time I stopped and failed to set them free. They didn't even like it when I stopped the car at red lights. Forget about shopping. I couldn't stop to look at anything. Freedom and movement is what they craved above all else and they were determined to get it.

That might not have been a problem if not for the needs of the older kids.

The school bus didn't come down our street, so I had two choices: walk the kids to the bus stop and fight constantly to keep the twins out of the road, out of the neighbors' lawns and out of the strollers of other parents; or take them into the school gym each day while I signed the older kids out and waited for them. It soon became clear that the gym was the safer alternative.

At first, all was good. We had to wait for the older kids, but the gym gave them ample space to run and play. Getting them to leave was a struggle, but I managed. Then they discovered the hallways. What a nightmare. I felt like I was the goalie in a fast-moving hockey game: always dodging to catch that puck before it passed through the net. Unfortunately, there was no net to stop them.

So I broke down.

I did the thing I thought I would never do: I bought backpack leashes. What a disaster.

Jonathan and Matthew loved them, of course. They were puppy backpacks and they were adorable. They wore them everywhere and they were quite proud. Until I touched that lead. As soon as I put my hand on it, they plunked themselves down and refused to move. They kicked and screamed and yelled.

They hollered and pushed and cried. They suddenly realized that these cool puppy backpacks were a means of control and they weren't having any of it.

After about five attempts, I gave up.

Instead, I struggled with them daily physically and mentally, suffering a shoulder injury that lasted more than a year. I hired babysitters for short trips and errands just to avoid that struggle, and I enlisted other parents who took pity on me. It was a tough year or two. I wanted nothing more than for Jonathan and Matthew to grow up.

Now, at almost four years old, they are fairly good about staying with me because they understand consequences and danger. They know now that if they stray from me, they might become lost or a stranger might take them away. They understand injury and pain and how much it might hurt if a car or a truck hit them.

But the past two years could have been much better. We could have gone more places, enjoyed more sights, done with a lot less yelling. I could even have had pain-free use of my shoulder if those harnesses had only worked for us.

I still cringe when I see a couple with no other children using one on a child at the mall, or when I see a child yanking another sibling on a harness, or when I see people who rely on them for every trip, everywhere never bothering to teach their children how to behave without them. I still think some people misuse them. But I now understand that there is a use for harnesses.

I no longer cringe at the thought of them. Instead of disgust, I am more likely to be filled with envy for those for whom harnesses worked. Thanks to Matthew and Jonathan, I have learned one very important lesson: Never say never.

DO IDENTICAL TWINS HAVE IDENTICAL SCENTS?

What if the worst happened? What if one of your identical twins disappeared or became lost? Could police dogs follow the scent of one identical twin without being confused by the other? Do identical twins have identical scents?

Until 2011, the answer was unclear.

Prior studies used dogs with various levels of training and failed to control such factors as the diets of the twin subjects (Certain foods, like garlic, can affect your body odor.). Sometimes the dogs could tell the difference between twins. Sometimes they could not.

Four scientists—Ludvík Pinc, Luděk Bartoš, Alice Reslová and Radim Kotrba—were determined to find out for sure. They used ten highly and equally trained German Shepherds and controlled the diets of their subjects (two sets of identical twins and two sets of fraternal twins, all children of similar ages) beforehand. Then they had the children wear squares of cotton for 20 minutes to absorb their body odors.

In an article published on June 15, 2011, in the journal *Plos One*, the scientists describe the results. The dogs were given individual scents and were ordered to select matches from among seven different jars. The jars included material worn by the other twin sibling to throw them off. Their handlers were kept in the dark about the details of the experiment. In each case, the dogs easily matched the scents of all the children, regardless of zygosity.

So the answer is, yes. Identical twins each have their own scent, but it might take a highly trained dog to sniff out the difference.

HAPPY BIRTHDAY, BOYS!

Four years

In an email exchange two years ago, I asked author/twin mom Susan Heim whether it gets easier as twins get older. Her boys were about four years old at the time. "It's doesn't really get easier," she said. "Just different."

I thought I understood and, the day after Matthew and Jonathan celebrated their second birthday, I wrote this:

All I could think about--honestly--is that two is halfway to four and that by four, they will be potty trained, they will respond to reason at some level, they will no longer need a stroller and they will talk in sentences. That doesn't mean I want to rush them. No, not at all.

I don't want them to grow up too fast. I adore their little kisses on my lips, cheeks and nose. I long for their tiny hands around my neck. I cherish their nonsensical exchanges that result in fits of giggles. And, wow. That unconditional trust only babies and toddlers have. That belief that mom is all-powerful, all-knowing, all-everything. That she is flawless. I see that in their eyes as they reach for me. They believe that I can make anything better. They really do.

No, I don't want to rush through that.

But they exhaust me lately as much as they exhilarate me.

And I find the exhaustion much easier to contend with if I have something to look forward to. So, on their birthday, while I was chasing them around the house trying desperately to persuade them to keep their clothes and diapers on at least until our neighbors arrived for cake and ice cream, I focused on the future.

I focused on how much easier it will become instead of thinking about how hard it sometimes has been. With that in mind, I found I could laugh at our little strippers and I caught them. They made it through the evening fully clothed.

Silly me. Jonathan and Matthew turned four today. It was an exciting day for me as well as for them. It was an emotional day. It was a trying day. It was exhausting. Wonderfully exhausting, and loaded with strong little hugs and kisses.

They sang. They danced. They fought over the birthday song. They hugged each other and pushed each other. They cried a bit. They laughed a lot. Just as I had hoped two birthdays before, they are fully potty trained. They understand reason on a fairly high level. They no longer need a stroller, and they carry on long and fascinating conversations.

They are amazing human beings and my heart aches each day they grow just a little bit older—each time they recognize the words "up" and "go" in books, each time they count on their little fingers, each time they create new, complicated games that include roles for me.

Part of me whimpers whenever they talk about their best friends: Jack for Jonathan; Adam for Matthew. I have to work hard to hold back when they want to put on their own clothes, cut their own food and ice skate on their own. They rarely even let me carry their sleds.

I relish the moments when we cuddle. I don't want to rush them. I really don't. But, as Susan said, four is not easier. It's just different. And, I have to admit, there is that little part of me that keeps saying, "Yippee! We're two-thirds of the way to six!"

IMAGINATION EXPLOSION

Four years

Just the other day, Matthew noticed a small embroidered palm tree on a beach towel. Within minutes, the towel was stretched across the floor and he and Jonathan were pirates, seeking lost treasures throughout the living room.

Only an hour earlier, they had been at the beach, wearing their swim trunks in the bathtub. Before that, I heard long tales about Dino Dan's impending visit. He was bringing his mother and his little brother and it was his birthday. Would I please bake a cake for him, they begged?

The day I have been waiting for has finally come.

Jonathan and Matthew have become so immersed in their imaginations that they often forget to wrestle, to pull the cushions off the sofa, to tear their beds apart, to dump water on the floor, to demand fruit treats, to tease the puppy, to tease their older siblings—to do all the little things they used to do when they were bored and wanted to stir things up.

It is still a lot of work.

I often have to provide props or act a part in their imaginary worlds. But that's OK. I would rather be the bad guy fighting Leonardo and Batman than the stressed-out mother who runs out of options and patience when time-outs don't work, and then yells far more than she ever wanted to.

Even better, their new-found manner of play allows their older brother and sister to take part. On Tuesday, when all four kids were stuck home for a snow day, they all played Pokemon together. The older kids loved the fact that the twins understood the show and they laughed whenever Matthew and Jonathan chose their Pokemons and unleashed them.

I wrote an entire chapter of my next novel that day. A whole chapter with all four kids at home. And I didn't feel guilty because they were all busy and all happy. We still have our moments and I'm sure we always will, but what a relief. What a huge, huge relief.

TWINS DIVIDED,
NATURALLY AND HAPPILY

Four years, one month

A new dynamic is moving through our house. Jonathan has ditched his twin brother as his best friend in favor of his older brother Riley, who is almost eleven. He draws pictures for him, fetches him Popsicles and emulates his every gesture, word and move when he is around. When Riley is in school or otherwise occupied, Jonathan turns back to Matthew again, taking up where he left off.

This worried me at first. How would Matthew handle the loss? My heart ached for him. Needlessly. As always, Matthew and Jonathan have surprised me. Matthew isn't the least bit bothered by Jonathan's new allegiance, no more so than he is bothered when Jonathan plays with other children in school. A comfort level seems to exits between the two of them that allows them to explore other relationships without diminishing their own.

I would like to believe that we have contributed to that confidence by never forcing them to separate. Yes, they have gone off on their own with my husband or me at different times, mostly on errands. Occasionally, for a bite to eat. But we have never felt the need to enroll them in different activities or classes simply to foster their individuality. We have never felt the need to tear them apart unnaturally.

Instead, they are teaching us to be patient, to step back and let them grow apart as we let them grow together. The pressure is on (always) from those who believe that forced separation is the only healthy way to raise identical twins. But forced separation is no healthier than forcing a shared identity through matching clothing, lumped nicknames or constantly calling attention to the fact that they are twins.

They are who they are.

And we love who they are.

We'll make mistakes along the way and plenty of them. But Jonathan's affection for Riley and Matthew's reaction to it have assured me that we are on the right track. And we have one very proud big brother, who is who amused and thrilled by his new status. For now.

FRIENDLY INDIFFERENCE

Four years, two months

I had always figured that Matthew and Jonathan's friends would easily be able to tell them apart. Isn't that part of the magic of childhood? This extra sense that kids have, the lack of filters that allow them to see things as they are?

So I was disappointed the other day at preschool when Matthew's best friend tapped Jonathan on the shoulder and called him by his brother's name. Jonathan ignored him except for the shrug indicating his annoyance at the constant interruption. I politely pointed out his mistake and directed him to Matthew who just right next to Jonathan. The boy gave me a puzzled look and then tapped Jonathan on the shoulder again.

"Matthew, Matthew. Come play," he said, his taps increasing in frequency. "Matthew."

I gave up. These are the things I worry about. It will be hard enough when adults mix them up as they grow older, but their friends? I recently read about a seven-year-old girl who was shunned by a group of her peers for no apparent reason. She later learned her identical twin sister had done something to upset them. They didn't change their stance when she explained the situation.

They chose not to differentiate between the two.

Jonathan and Matthew enjoy having different friends, though they all play together nicely. I hope this boy is an exception. Another friend, the one Jonathan claims as his closest, tries. He doesn't always get it right, but he at least makes an effort. If he is unsure, he figures it out within few minutes of play. A little girl who greets us daily when we enter the classroom always asks me who is who first thing. She wants to be clear. She's always felt that need to know who is who.

I haven't paid enough attention to the others.

I have told the boys over and over again that people will mix them up and that they should forgive them. Simply correct them and forgive them. But I think I might have to revise that tutorial when they outgrow preschool and begin their elementary years.

We all make mistakes. People will mix them up. But if they are not sure, they should ask. And if Matthew and Jonathan politely correct them, they should apologize and make an effort in the future. I guess all I'm asking for is an effort.

Try to see Matthew.
Try to see Jonathan.
They are two boys, not one.

DIFFERENCE AND EMPATHY

Four years, three months

As I slipped a new shirt over Matthew's head for preschool pictures the other day, he said, "Is this my own, mom? Can it be my own?"

"Of course," I answered.

"Not Jon's?"

'Not Jon's."

"Just my own?"

"Just your own."

"Thanks, mom, for letting it be my own."

And Jonathan did not protest.

Moments later, a teacher asked whether Mathew and Jonathan would be sitting together for their photo like the other set of twins in the class or whether they wanted to take them separately. Jonathan barely let her finish the question.

"Separate," he yelled. "I want my own."

Matthew did not argue.

"My own" has been the mantra in our household lately.

Matthew and Jonathan have always had their independent streaks. They have always had their own favorite colors, their own sides of the minivan, their own scooters, their own favorite foods and their own special stuffed animals.

But lately, we're seeing a different kind of independence, a gentler sort that seems to develop in conjunction with something else: empathy. The more Matthew and Jonathan strive to differentiate from each other, the more attentive they are to each other, and the more concerned they are with the other's needs.

While each boy had his picture taken, the other watched. They cheered each other on, encouraged each other to smile and told each other they'd made a good picture. Matthew won't get out of bed most mornings until Jonathan sings him the preschool "good morning" song and Jonathan obliges. Jonathan got angry with me the other day because he felt the jacket I'd given Matthew wasn't warm enough. Matthew gave up the Spiderman pajamas two nights ago because Jonathan wanted them so badly.

When one gets a Popsicle from the freezer, he gets one for the other—in his favorite flavor.

When they were babies, I had always thought their similarities would be the foundation of their bond. Now, I'm seeing it in a new light. Their differences and their mutual respect for that desire for difference are just as important. They have their moments. They are siblings, after all, and they are with each other nearly 24 hours a day. Injuries happen. Harsh words are exchanged. A lot.

But more times than not, I find myself listening to their exchanges from behind a corner—eavesdropping—and wondering what to do with all that pride that's swelling inside me. They amaze me and intrigue me. Every single day.

BATTLE OF THE HEIGHTS: AN UNWINNABLE GAME

Four years, four months

We had an all-out brawl in our household the other day. Fists were flying. Legs were kicking. Bodies were thrown to the floor. It started when I noticed Matthew and Jonathan had grown. I stood them up against a kitchen wall and marked their heights with a pen. My mistake?

"Look," I said, pointing to the lines on the wall. "You are exactly the same height again."

The reaction was simultaneous.

"I'm taller," they announced.

"No, I'm taller," they growled together.

"I am the winner," they screamed into each other's faces with fists balled at their sides.

I tried to speak. I tried to intervene. But, within seconds, the verbal battle had turned physical—intensely physical. And each time I tried to break it up, I simply got pummeled by both. In my panic, in my frustration, in my anger, I screamed:

"Stop! Now! You are identical twins! You were born the same height. You will always, forever and ever, be the same height!"

First, they stared at me -- stopped and stared. Then those wide eyes, both sets of them, filled with tears. Finally, the tears fell and sobs shook their very tall bodies. I got down on my knees and pulled them both close, hugging one with each arm. I explained to them, or tried to, that their shared height, foot size and hand size were among the things that made them extra special. They weren't buying it. So I chose another tactic.

"You are both huge," I said. "When somebody tries to pick on a little kid and the two of you stand in front of him, cross your arms over your chest (I stood and demonstrated.) and tell him to leave that kid alone, what do you think he's going to do?"

"Go away," Jonathan yelled.

"Say, 'sorry'," said Matthew.

"Together, you're pretty scary," I assured them.

With that, our talk disintegrated—into a game of monsters.

Their shared-height crisis was, at least for the moment, forgotten.

WHO WAS BORN FIRST

Four years, five months

Matthew and Jonathan are competitive. Very competitive. For that reason, there is one question I dread more than any other. One question that has not yet occurred to them. One question that will, inevitably, come up.

Who was born first?

I have an answer, a clever one. "It doesn't matter who was born first," I will say, "because you were conceived at precisely the same moment."

No doubt about it. Jonathan and Matthew started life as one and then became two simultaneously. They have existed for precisely the same amount of time. So why should it matter who hung out in my uterus for an extra twenty minutes or so, doing the breath stroke, a little freestyle and maybe even the butterfly? One got a little more experience with the outside world while the other experienced freedom in the womb, something his twin will never know. Even-Steven. Logical, right? I can see their reactions now.

Silence. For a moment. A placid look, one of contemplation. The one time when they truly look identical. Then their faces will scrunch up and the nature of that scrunch will change quickly, from cute to annoyed to angry, expressions greatly affected by the amount of padding in each twins' cheeks, the slightly narrower bone structure of one twin's face and the different ways in which they have trained their facial muscles over the years.

It will be one of those times when I truly wonder whether the DNA tests were right, whether they really are identical. And when I see those expressions, I can think of only one way to react. The only reasonable solution. My salvation.

"Go ask dad," I'll say.

"Just go ask dad."

UPDATE: HOW THEY REACTED

It's an easy ice-breaker. People will stare at twins and, as a quick conversation starter, they will often ask, "Which of you was born first?" We can never predict who will ask them or when, so it was impossible to protect them from the subject of birth order forever.

Thankfully, our plan worked.

Each time it came up, we explained how identical twins form, how Matthew and Jonathan became individuals at precisely the same moment. The only difference, we told them, is that one left the womb a few minutes earlier while the other enjoyed have the room to himself for a while.

Now, when people ask, they will answer that Matthew was the first-born, but they have no further interest in the conversations. If adults pursue it, they are likely to get detailed lessons in how babies are made. That is usually enough to put an end to it.

FRATERNAL VS. IDENTICAL: THE ATTENTION FACTOR

Four years, six months

It's rare, but it happens.

Most often, parents of fraternal twins find the fact that Matthew and Jonathan are identical interesting, but it ends there. Raising identical twins has its unique challenges, but parents of any category of twins have so much in common that further discussion of their zygosity needn't come up.

But every now and then, I'll get that immediate snub from a fraternal-twin parent, that kind of look that I'd expect to see on a middle school playground from the girl who is envious of the other girl for reasons that are all in her own head.

I know what that look means because I am a curious person. I've explored it before. I've pushed past the snub and pursued conversations. It means that this parent is a little envious because she believes my twins get more attention than hers.

The hard part is that she is probably right.

The harder part is that it shouldn't matter.

The people we meet don't mean to upset anybody and it certainly doesn't mean that fraternal twins are any less valued. It's just that identical twins are more obvious. They attract attention. But, as we were often taught during sensitivity training in my former career as a journalist, intention is pretty much meaningless. Perception is what counts.

Reporter Dionne Searcey of The Wall Street Journal gathered these sentiments at the Twins Days festival in Twinsburg, Ohio, for her Aug. 9, 2011 article, *At a Convention Full of Them, It's Apparent Not All Twins are Created Equal*:

"I feel shafted here because everybody looks the same."

"Yeah, we're the redheaded stepchild here, the fraternals."

"Nobody ever asks us if we're twins."

"There's a caste system for twins, and identicals are in the upper caste."

I'm not sure what the solution is other than to be respectful of those feelings and to validate them. Take as much of an interest in their twins as people take in ours. One mom in the article didn't have her twins tested even though they look very much alike. "I don't think it's important," she told the reporter, "and I don't think it matters."

RAISING THE CURTAIN ON DRAMATIC PLAY

Four years, seven months

I was walking past Matthew and Jonathan's bedroom the other day when I heard this:

"Get out of my room, you two! I said, get out now!"

"But we just want to play."

"Get out!"

I paused just outside the doorway and peeked in.

It was just the two of them, playing with the dollhouse their older sister had given them. Apparently, identical train engines Bill and Ben were invading their sister's bedroom. Their sister, a soft lavender engine, named Rosie, was livid. The engines whimpered away, muttering "Bossy boiler."

Hmmm.

That plot sounded familiar.

Matthew and Jonathan have been acting out many familiar scenarios lately and they've spent even more time coming up with new ones. Sometimes they are at a huge splash park and each room is a different pool or slide or ride. Other times, they are airplanes and they are flying to visit various relatives with a particular interest in the relatives' dogs. Quite often, super heroes, game show hosts and the Road Runner and Wile E. Coyote make appearances in our household as well.

Dramatic play rules these days and it's a mixed blessing.

It is fantastic to watch them play. Their games are seamless, each twin's actions and dialogue perfectly following the other's. They'll stick with one imaginative scenario for an hour or more and I can go happily about my housework or writing. These guys click. They really click.

But when it falls apart, the explosion is equally intense.

It is advisable to take shelter. I have learned that trains can fly. I have learned that there is a price to pay for my free time. I have learned that disciplining identical twins and mediating their arguments is a huge time and energy drain, stealing back all those gains I might have made earlier in the day. Their level of engagement with each other is so intense that they have a long way to fall when they let each other go.

The cool thing, though, is that they always recover fully.

Their older brother and sister played together well, too, at their ages. Riley would pull out his dinosaurs and Kiersten would bring her Polly Pockets into the living room. Together, they would build huge cities that would remain sprawled across on the floor for days on end, providing hours' worth of entertainment.

But as they have grown, their differences have grown, too.

Riley and Kiersten are still close at ages 10 and 11.

Just not in the same way.

But this thing with Jonathan and Matthew is a little bit different.

Riley and Kiersten had to talk about what they were going to do. They had to plan, bargain, negotiate, agree. They did it well, but the need was still there. They negotiated endings, too, each telling the other a few minutes beforehand that he or she was going to quit (at mom's insistence after many an argument).

Not so for Jonathan and Matthew.

When they start an imaginative game, it just happens and it flows naturally, smoothly, without guiding words. When they decide to move on to something else, it just happens, too. They either play another game without missing a beat or each wanders off on his own.

Watching Matthew and Jonathan play together can be exhausting and exhilarating at the same time, particularly with their high energy levels. The anticipation of the potential explosion—often caused by one claiming the other's coveted train engine—can be stressful, very stressful, enough to undo all the work I've done to bring my blood pressure down.

But like anything else that is exciting, dangerous and beautiful all at the same time, it is worth it.

TOGETHER IN THE CLASSROOM

Four years, eight months

So far, so good. Matthew and Jonathan are attending two different full-day preschools this year. Together. On Mondays and Wednesdays, they attend a private preschool with a class size of seven to thirteen, depending on the day. They go to the public preschool Tuesdays and Thursdays with a total of sixteen kids in their classroom and sixteen in the other.

The reasons they attend two schools are complicated, but the results are interesting.

Their overall behaviors vary from school to school because of the differences in structure, but in both schools, the teachers say they play separately with different friends and come together only when they are tired. They do share friends, but they play with them at different times. They don't cry when they are dropped off. They barely say good-bye. They are comfortable. They are well-adjusted. And there is no doubt they are behaving like individuals.

This is important because of all the naysayers, the people who insist that all twins should be separated in school. We are fortunate in that administrators in both schools seem to be firmly against any such blanket policies.

At the public preschool, which is run by the county's Head Start program but accepts kids from all income levels, the administrator I spoke with was already aware of the studies that show identical twins generally fare better psychologically and academically when they are place together in the early years.

She believes that most twins should stay together early on unless the parents have a firm opposition to it. So many parents want their kids in classes with their best friends so they will be more comfortable, she noted. Why would it be different for twins who take comfort in each other's company?

At the private school, there is only one classroom, so we had no choice. No big deal.

No one even brought it up.

We will pay close attention to Jonathan and Matthew as they move through the levels of elementary school. We will watch for any issues that indicate they need separation and, as they get older, we will ask them at the end of each year what their preferences are for the next year. But until or unless we see any reason to separate them, we will not.

Why would we?

SCIENTISTS FIND IDENTICAL TWINS PERCEIVE THE WORLD IN NEARLY IDENTICAL WAYS

In a study that might change the way the medical community treats autism and similar disorders, scientists have found that how children perceive the world—what they look at, and what they don't—is genetically influenced.

And once again, we have identical twins to thank.

A study reported July 12, 2017, by Washington University School of Medicine in St. Louis and Emory University School of Medicine in Atlanta tracked the eye movements of 338 children ages 18 months to 24 months old. The study group included identical twins, fraternal twins, children with autism and a control group of 84 singletons.

They were tested with and without their parents present. Their eye movements were tracked while they watched videos of common childhood scenes, such as children at play or actresses playing the role of a caregiver. The scientists separated identical and fraternal twins from their siblings during the viewings.

They were tested again a year later.

The results were the same for both years. Fraternal twins were attracted to the same objects or faces only 10 percent of the time. For identical twins, however, the way they perceived the videos was nearly 100 percent identical. If one focused on faces and eyes first, so did the other. If one noticed objects first, so did the other.

Identical twins were also more likely to move their eyes at the same moments in time, in the same directions, towards the same locations and the same content, mirroring one another's behavior to within as little as 17 milliseconds, according to the study.

In children with autism, the match levels were so far below 10 percent, that scientists believe they can mathematically identify children in the study who have autism. This could lead to earlier diagnosis and new opportunities for invention for children with autism. Perhaps if we can change the way they see the world, we can help them become a more active part of it.

HOLIDAY GIFTS FOR IDENTICAL TWINS: THE SAME OR DIFFERENT?

Four years, ten months

Each year as the holidays approach, the same question appears on the online forums for parents of twins. Parents want to know whether they should buy identical gifts, matching gifts or different gifts for their same-aged children.

For certain items, it's obvious: if you buy a bike for one twin, you should buy a bike for the other. For boy/girl twins, it gets easier as they get older thanks to social coding: a seven-year-old girl is likely to want Polly Pockets while a seven-year-old boy might want a Bionicle. But they will both probably want iPhones someday. Some same-sex fraternal twins make it easy, too, if they have entirely different interests.

But identical twins present a different challenge.

As parents, we have to recognize their shared DNA also means predominately shared brain chemistry. Their talents, skills and general interests tend to be the same or, at least, very similar. They also have the same body types, which might naturally lead them to similar physical pursuits.

At the same time, identical twins have choices about which talents, skills, interests and physical pursuits to cultivate. Those choices along with environmental influences help them develop as individuals with sometimes differing needs and wants.

So how does that translate into a holiday shopping list?

In the beginning, err on the side of caution. Babies are babies. They don't know how to share and they really don't care whether you want them to. Buy two of the same when it is appropriate to buy more than one of a particular item.

Don't do what we did.

We made the mistake of buying Matthew a yellow Animal Alley Good-Night bear for his crib when the twins were babies. We bought Jonathan the floppy-eared, blue Good-Night puppy (which we thought, until recently, was a rabbit!). The animals were equally soft and similar in shape. We never thought they'd care.

We were wrong.

By four months old, they were already fighting over a toy. They both wanted that yellow bear in bed with them and they would scream and cry until they got it. An emergency trip to Toy-R-Us resolved the problem, but it was a long time before I made that mistake again.

By sixteen months old, the boys had developed definite color preferences of their own. At this point, we could buy them the same toys, but in different colors. Jonathan got the blue dinosaur while Matthew got the green one. Matthew got the red truck while Jonathan got the orange one.

Everybody was happy.

There was no point in forcing entirely different toys on them. They wanted the same things and they were happy with the same things. We wanted to give our children gifts that they would enjoy, that made them happy. Receiving the same gifts in different colors made them happy.

But that stage doesn't last forever.

Even the closest of identical twins eventually differentiate, at least in the eyes of those who are paying attention. And that differentiation can make holiday shopping more challenging and more satisfying. We are just beginning to see those changes in our guys at four years old.

Matthew and Jonathan still enjoy the same general things, like trains… and more trains… and more trains. Did I mention they like trains? And movies about trains? And train T-shirts? And books about trains? And anything at all related to trains?

But, this year, they want different engines.

Matthew wants 'Arry and Burt of the *Thomas the Tank Engine* fame while Jonathan wants Neville and Isobella. They both want the wooden Tidmouth sheds, so Santa will probably give that as a combined gift. They'll get some games they can play together and lots of books that each can call his own. Jonathan might get a new basketball, his biggest sports obsession, but Matthew has no interest in that. Matthew would likely prefer more Legos.

And, well, that's probably about it for now.

They have plenty of different food preferences and they like different textures of clothing, but toys are for playing together at their age and they love playing together. So they tend to love the same types of toys.

And the holidays, for four-year-olds, are all about toys.

I am anticipating more differences when gifts involve clothing, iTunes and Wii games.

Forcing identical twins to accept different toys will not foster individuality. Nor will forcing them to accept the same toys somehow make them inseparable. It's natural for them to lean the same way and it's natural for them to want to be a little bit different.

Gift shopping for identical twins is a challenge, but the challenge is simply one of concentration, of focusing on the minutia. It takes more energy to find those differences and similarities that make gifts for identical twins the perfect gifts.

But, otherwise, it is really no different than it is for other children.

And the thrill on their faces—that thrill they share first with their twin as they rip off the paper and expose the treasure inside and then with their siblings and with us—makes all that extra energy well worth the effort.

WANT ATTENTION? DRESS THEM ALIKE

Four years, eleven months

It's rare that our twins are dressed alike. Sure, we did it now and then when they were babies. It was cute, especially for photos. But it confused us and others and, as soon as they were able to grunt in the direction of a particular piece of clothing, Matthew and Jonathan made their own preferences clear. At this point in their lives, they find the idea of dressing alike generally repulsive.

So it was by mistake that it happened last week.

We were headed out to Target and the mall, intending to do some Christmas shopping and meet up with a friend for pictures with Santa. Neither twin wanted to wear his jacket. I agreed only if they each grabbed a sweater. They grabbed precisely the same ones. Coincidentally, they were both wearing gray sweatpants of slightly different shades.

I didn't think much of it until we entered Target.

Most often, passersby don't even realize Jonathan and Matthew are twins. I always assumed that we had naturally passed the phase where people cared—when they were babies, sitting side-by-side in their stroller announcing their identical DNA to the world.

Babyhood was tough. I always had to build in extra time for oglers. I didn't mind much because the twins were too young to understand that they were a side show of sorts. Besides, they made people happy. It was nice to see previously frowning folks stop and smile. But I should have built it in extra time that day.

It started the moment we entered. Two women walking toward us stopped, blocking our way. They stared at the twins, slightly stooped for a better angle, looking them up and down. Then they stood up straight and one woman said with a bit of a puzzled look, "Are they twins?"

"Yes," I answered.

"I knew it," said one.

"Me too," said the other, and the two women carried on a conversation about Matthew and Jonathan's likenesses and differences as though none of us was there. I maneuvered the twins around them and kept walking.

Once we grabbed a cart and the twins were walking freely, not holding my hands, I figured we were safe. Certainly, no one would stop us if they were not on display side-by-side and if we looked really busy. Would they?

They would.

Similar incidents occurred at least six more times during our forty-minute shopping excursion. Some people were polite and brief. Others were a little more intrigued, yet still polite. No one else was rude like those two women. Shoppers just seemed attracted by their twinness, like they couldn't help themselves, and I found that kind of amusing.

When we left Target and arrived at the mall, Jonathan stripped off his sweater.

He was hot.

Matthew kept his on.

We attracted not a single comment or stare during our ninety-minute trek through the halls, food court and arcade. (OK, maybe a stare, but that probably had more to do with the rather "active" behaviors of Matthew and Jonathan and their preschool-aged friend.) Not even Santa noticed. At least, not until we were preparing to leave and Jonathan pulled on his sweater.

Their friend was gone by then, so it was just the two boys standing there, waiting for me to get my act together. Santa had risen from his chair and was greeting children in the common area a few yards away. He looked at Jonathan and Matthew, who caught his stare and galloped over. Santa gazed at them, and then lifted his eyes to me.

"Are they twins?" he said.

I swear I saw a mischievous twinkle.

ONE BIRTHDAY CAKE OR TWO? AN UNNECESSARY STRESS

Four years, eleven months

I have some advice for parents who fret over whether their twins should have one birthday cake or two, one birthday song or two, one birthday theme or two. Forget it. Who cares? They don't. Not at one and two years old. Honestly. Don't be embarrassed.

We've all been there, thinking the wrong decision, the wrong move will forever scar our little babies and toddlers, particularly since they already share looks and DNA. How will they ever become individuals if we make them celebrate their shared birthdays as units?

As Matthew and Jonathan approach their fifth birthday, I can assure you that when it matters, they will tell you. They will tell you over and over and over again until you instinctively cringe whenever the topic comes up and make elaborate attempts at distraction.

For us, it started with cakes at three years old.

Matthew made it clear to me that his cake should have yellow frosting. Jonathan wanted blue. They also wanted their own versions of the birthday song. They stressed these points with anyone who would listen for weeks prior to their birthday. That was it. We complied and they were happy.

Their fourth birthday was a yearlong obsession. They understood, for the first time, what a birthday meant, and the excitement overwhelmed them. Over the preceding months, we made cakes for Dino Dan, for Dora, and for the dog. We celebrated on picnic blankets on the living floor, with paper plates on the dining room table and at Friendly's with the Birthday Bash dessert. It seemed birthdays were all they thought about.

They started planning a full year in advance. Jonathan requested a chocolate cake with blue frosting and Matthew asked for a banana cake with yellow frosting. They wanted separate birthday songs once again and they knew exactly who they wanted to invite. No more family-only parties. They wanted the real thing with lots of friends.

We complied and, again, they were happy.

This year, the plans are even more elaborate. They attend two different preschools together (two days at one and two days at the other). I had planned to bring treats only to the school they attend on their actual birthday. Not fair, they said, not fair to their other friends. Fine, I said. They won.

So I decided to bring only one treat to each class, certain the teachers would appreciate limitations on sugar consumption. Not fair, they argued once again. Jonathan and Matthew are two different people, each with his own birthday. They should each be able to bring a treat. How could I possibly argue with that?

I agreed, but only for the one classroom.

In the other class, we will bring drinks and a treat.

Their party requests are the same at the previous year—specific colors and flavors for cakes, separate songs and lots of friends. Thank goodness the community center is cheap. But they added one more thing this year—piñatas. Not one, but two. They used the same logic in support of their argument: two birthdays, two piñatas.

Ugh.

I had dug my own hole by caving to this premise before. Two piñatas it is. We will comply and they will be happy.

I can't even imagine what their sixth birthday will be like, but I'm already starting to work on it, planning my arguments for less separation, less individualism, more focus on the fact that their shared birthday is part of what makes their relationship so special. Yes, it's a selfish argument, but we have to draw the line somewhere before they drive us into financial ruin. We will not entirely comply, but they will be happy.

So my advice is to relax.

Children who can barely form sentences have little or no concept of what a birthday is so much for whether a joint celebration defines them as a unit. Their birthdays will present enough opportunities for stress in the years to come.

PART 4

Ready for Kindergarten

(Ages 5 to 6 years)

Oh, my nerves! Matthew and Jonathan would soon be going to kindergarten. Was the world ready for them? Were the twins ready for the world? Jonathan and Matthew were preschool veterans. Their years of classroom experience should have made the transition to kindergarten easy, but it wasn't. Well, it was a breeze for them. I was the one stressing out. In preschool, I could send them or keep them home at will. I could dictate which class they would be in and enroll them elsewhere if I sensed they were unhappy or were not getting the social and emotion guidance we'd sought. They attended for just a few hours a week, whatever made me comfortable. Preschool was a service we paid for. We were customers with the power of choice. But kindergarten was a whole new realm.

I worried whether the foundation they'd built in the early years would hold up under the social and academic pressures of the public school environment. I worried that people would treat them as a unit, but I also worried about preserving their unique bond. I worried about whether we were making the right decision in keeping them together and whether I would have to defend that decision for years to come. It was a huge leap toward independence for the twins and a new experience in both trust and in advocacy for me.

But I had worried for naught.

Both boys have thrived in school. They have maintained their bond while developing friendships of their own. They separated in first grade so one twin could work on some emotional issues without negatively affecting the other. But they are together about half the day in reading groups, recess and gym. The boys like having their own teachers, but they look forward to their time together. In our tiny school district, the similarities in their academic performances will land them in the same classes from seventh grade on. They are enjoying their half days of independence from each other while they can.

My advice to you? Keep in mind that you know your twins better than anyone. Read the studies on school placement for twins, listen to the advice of those who work in the academic environment, and observe how your twins react to their new situations. But, when in doubt, go with your gut. Choose the paths that make sense for your unique set of identical twins. Each twin is unique and each bond between twins is unique. Just as no two people are alike, no two sets of identical twins are alike. You are the expert on your own children. Remember that.

SICK AND SICKER: IMMUNITY DIFFERENCES IN IDENTICAL TWINS

Five years

Jonathan and Matthew developed colds a while back. Jonathan is on the mend now, racing the dog from the dining room through the kitchen, eating like a teenager and jumping from the sofa to the floor over and over and over again, ignoring my demands that he stop. He's driving me crazy.

Matthew is curled up on another sofa, covered with a blanket and watching TV through half-opened eyes. It breaks my heart to watch him hold his ribs when hacking coughs overtake his body. I can't wait for the antibiotics to do their stuff. He has walking pneumonia.

This medical inequity is nothing new.

A few weeks ago, Jonathan developed a fever that lasted for two days. Matthew caught the same virus, but his fever continued for seven days. A stomach bug that left Jonathan slightly dehydrated for a day as a baby left Matthew with bleeding ulcers and a month's prescription of Zantac. When Jonathan develops an ear infection, Matthew often gets it in both.

My immediate reaction was to surmise that somehow, when the egg split, Matthew lost an immunity gene to Jonathan. It made sense. Matthew's always been sicker and he was born lighter, slighter—a tiny bit frailer than his brother. But I came to a different conclusion after doing a little research.

Recent studies are finding that epigenetics—or the way in which genes express themselves in different environments—is likely responsible for many differences that develop in identical twins, particularly when it comes to immunity. Sometime after conception, either in the womb or outside it, one of the twins was likely exposed to a virus or bacteria that missed the other. In fighting off the intruder, he either gained an army (Jonathan), strengthening his physical fortress, or lost one (Matthew), weakening his defenses. Their identical genes learned to express themselves in different ways when confronted by bacterial infections or viruses, resulting in permanently different immune systems.

Amanda Carpenter, a virology student, writes about an excellent example in her May, 5, 2011, post on Virology Blog: About Viruses and Viral Disease (http://www.virology.ws). Identical twins born in 1983 were exposed to HIV, the virus that causes AIDS. Fifteen years later, one was relatively healthy and strong while the other was sickly and ill. After studying blood samples from the pair, researchers concluded environment, which led to a depressed immunity system in one twin, was likely to blame for their different reactions. Their shared DNA did not ensure a shared prognosis.

My hope for Matthew is that someday this will turn itself around—that someday he'll be exposed to something that makes him stronger instead or weaker—and that Jonathan's immunity will remain unchanged. Who knows? Maybe this is the one. Maybe all that hacking and coughing that kept me up last night, worried that he will choke or stop breathing, is the just influence his genes need.

DOCTORS OFTEN MISINFORM PARENTS ABOUT ZIGOSITY

Five years, one month

Throughout my pregnancy, my OB and the ultrasound technician told us our boys were absolutely, positively, no-doubt-about-it fraternal. Yes, my doctor said, identicals can have separate placentas and sacs, but mine implanted too far apart to be identical. Their placentas were on polar opposite sides of the uterus. Identical twins implant more closely, he said.

He was wrong.

And he has company.

In a 2012 study published in the journal BJOG, University College London, researchers found doctors wrongly told parents their identical twins were fraternal in 27.5 percent of the cases. Like my guys, those twins had their own sacs and placentas.

The study also found that 2 percent of parents were wrongly told their fraternal twins were identical because doctors did not realize their separate placentas had fused into one. Overall, 15 percent of twin parents were misinformed about zygosity.

I have long suspected the statistics involving identical twins are skewed. This proves it.

So many parents find out long after birth their supposedly fraternal twins are identical through DNA testing. That information is never reported to any statistic-gathering source. If this study hold true in the United States, then statistics showing the odds of having identical twins is about 3 in 1,000 are way off.

It has become a game on online twin forums: Guess whether the twins are identical while the parents await results of DNA testing. In most every case where parents of di/di (separate sacs and placentas) had trouble telling their twins apart, the results showed they were, indeed, monozygotic, or identical.

I have come across just as many parents of look-alike twins in real life and who decline testing despite their gut feelings. Either they can't afford the $100 to $200 fee or they see slight differences between their twins and accept those as evidence their twins are fraternal. We could have done that with our guys.

Matthew has a slighter build and a thinner face. Jonathan is much more muscular and has a rounded face—a little more body fat in his cheeks. But that scenario is true of most identicals. One usually has a slightly different facial shape than the other. In some of those cases, parents brushed off their identical suspicions because their hospitals "tested" the placentas and the results showed they were dizygotic, or fraternal. Our own doctor fell for that until I pressed him for more information and he checked with the hospital.

It turns out hospitals, in general, check only whether placentas are fused. The hospital techs either definitively declare the zygosity according to the results or they pass the results on to doctors or midwives who were told in medical school that two placentas equals fraternal. The doctors or midwives then pass that misinformation on to parents.

Remember this: hospitals DO NOT do DNA testing.

In the defense of OBs, midwives and ultrasound technician, zygosity is irrelevant in caring for pregnant women and their babies. What matters is only whether there is one placenta or two, and one sac or two. So they really don't need to know for medical purposes. That doesn't, however, excuse the giving of misinformation.

In our case, a fellow soccer mom who was a neonatologist educated me.

She told me identical twins implant separately when the split occurs immediately after conception—within the first few days. Matthew and Jonathan probably became two babies usually far up in the fallopian tube, she said, allowing them to fall and implant independently, just like fraternal twins.

At the very least, our OB should have told us he didn't know.

He should have known that he didn't know.

All doctors, midwives and ultrasound technicians should know they can't be certain with same-gender twins until after the babies are born. Though the information is medically irrelevant during pregnancy, there is no excuse for being misinformed about something so relevant to the field in general or for passing that information on to parents. None.

AND SO IT BEGINS...

Five years, three months

Matthew and Jonathan rarely dress alike, but their Angry Birds shirts are new (a gift from their big sister) and they are obsessed, so each insisted on wearing his this morning.

As Matthew was dressing, his face suddenly burst into a grin.

"Let's wear the same pants, too, so we can trick the teachers," he said with a giggle. "I'll say I'm Jon and he'll say he's Matt!"

I refused, of course, but the idea lived on.

Matthew dreamed up all kinds of scenarios that involved fooling people with their similarities. Jonathan was less intrigued, but willing to go along with his brother's plans.

Thankfully, they forgot about the whole thing when they arrived at school to find another child in an Angry Birds shirt.

Angry Bird talk dominated instead.

They cannot fool me and I honestly doubt they look enough alike to pull it off with the teachers who know them best, but the seed is germinating despite our efforts to make conditions unfavorable.

And who can blame them?

While the parent in me growls at the thought, the kid in me is a bit envious.

Life can be tough as an identical twin, so I understand why they might want to have a little fun with it once in a while, especially since this is something only identical twins can do.

But it would be unfair to their teachers and their friends, and it would be awfully hard for them to demand treatment as individuals if they acted like a unit even just for a day.

So the foot is down.

The fun is quashed.

For now.

At least until they are old enough and clever enough to defy me.

SEPARATE BEDROOMS: ADDRESSING THE ISSUE BY DESIGN

Five years, four months

Right now, our boys enjoy sharing a bedroom. They face each other as they fall asleep. They often decline to snuggle in our bed when they awaken at night because neither wants to leave the other alone in his room. They look for each other and, usually, wake each other as soon as the sun rises.

But we know that will end someday.

We know it should end someday.

So this left us with a dilemma as we approached the architect who will design our next house, our final house, we hope. A timber frame hybrid on a hill surrounded by fields and woods. A place to write in peace. A pantry. A mud room. A place that… OK, I'm getting off track. I'm just a little excited.

At five years old, Matthew and Jonathan will still bunk together when we eventually move in, but they will probably want to separate before the older kids move out. In talking both virtually and in person with identical twin boys and parents of identical twin boys, I have found the average age for bedroom separation requests is junior high—seventh or eighth grade. Since we are starting from scratch with this house, we have the opportunity to address the issue in our design.

We pondered moving one twin into the basement, but not for long. I don't like the idea. I find peace in knowing all my kids are together on one floor. I also worry that Jonathan and Matthew will waiver in their insistence at separating, wanting their own rooms one minute and whining for togetherness the next. I have visions of furniture making multiple trips up and down stairs and across hallways and back, and kids sneaking up and down stairs in the middle of the night. No, that wouldn't work.

So we thought and thought and thought. Then we thought some more. Finally, we came up with a solution: two separate bedrooms of equal size with wide, pocket doors between them. The architect sent the preliminary sketches this weekend and we showed them to the twins. They were thrilled.

When we first move in, Jonathan and Matthew will sleep in one room. Their dressers and some of their toys will be in the other room and the doors will remain open. The doors can stay open when they move into their own rooms, allowing them to check on each other or holler to each other when or if they are nervous. Matthew and Jonathan can take the initiative to shut them when they are ready. Our hope is that they will easily and naturally work their way apart when the time is right.

And, yes, we realize it will not always be smooth-going. We'll have plenty of ice packs available for the fingers, toes and limbs that will likely fall victim to those pocket doors as identical adolescent hormones rage. But the twins are five now and I choose not to think about that. Instead, I'm thinking about hardwood floors, trusses, great rooms and coffee at sunrise on a wrap-around porch.

BEDROOM UPDATE

At about eight years old, Matthew and Jonathan decided they wanted separate rooms. One twin or the other had pushed the move a few times, but this was the first time both boys were on board. So we did it.

The transition has been peaceful. Sometimes they keep the pocket door open. Sometimes they close it. Every now and then, they have a sleep over in one twin's room. For the most part, they seem to respect each other's boundaries and privacy.

The pocket door design paid off.

UGH! TIME FOR SCOWLING LESSONS?
Five years, four months

I got a rare glimpse yesterday into the minds of Matthew and Jonathan and how they experience the world as identical twins. We were sitting in the minivan after a school field trip, waiting for their older brother and sister to emerge from the school building. A friend passed by with her twin boys, who are two years younger than our guys. I opened the sliding van door so Matthew and Jonathan could see the other twins and say, "Hello."

My friend's twins both have the same hue of bright blond hair, the same fair skin and are about the same height. But one of her boys has curls and an outgoing, social personality. The other has straighter hair and is more clingy, more cautious in his approach. Though they are obviously brothers, I've never had trouble telling them apart. They are clearly fraternal.

After the other twins left, a conversation ensued in the back seat.

Jonathan: "I can't tell them apart. That's why I don't use their names."

Matthew: "Yes, they look the same to me."

Jonathan: "At least they weren't dressed the same. That helps."

Matthew: "I think one has a fuller face. I still can't tell them apart though."

I was stunned. I wasn't sure whether to laugh or cry. How many times had they heard this? How many people have examined Jonathan and Matthew and spoken of them—right in front of them—as if they were simply objects, highly insensitive with their games of "What makes these pictures different?" This back-seat conversation was clearly not about the twin friends we'd just seen. Matthew and Jonathan were emulating adult conversations, conversations they'd overheard.

This happened frequently when they were babies and toddlers. I didn't worry then because I figured Matthew and Jonathan couldn't comprehend it anyway. They were immersed in their own, egocentric worlds. But as they got older, I started to hush people when the comparisons began. Then, when they got a lot older, I started to scowl. Soon it seemed that people had gotten smarter. They still compared the boys. That's only natural. Heck, I do it, too. But they compared them out of earshot.

I guess the reactions to my scowls misled me. I'd thought things had gotten better recently, that the overt and callus comparisons had become less frequent, especially since Matthew and Jonathan rarely even wear the same shirts, have tried to achieve different haircuts, have developed such different personalities, and have different amounts of fullness in their faces making their expressions unique. I guess I was wrong.

Jonathan and Matthew are out of my hands more often nowadays. They are in preschool four days a week, where they interact not only with teachers, but with parents of other children. Teachers tend to be sensitive, but that doesn't ensure that other adults they encounter will be. Sigh.

I've taught Jonathan and Matthew to be upfront when people are unsure who is who and tell them their names. Right now, they aren't bothered by that. I've tried to help them understand that it's not an insult. People just need help sometimes because they look so much alike on the outside. I guess we need another lesson though. I guess I need to teach them how to scowl.

DIFFERENTIATION IN IDENTICAL SIBLINGS BEGINS BEFORE BIRTH

Five years, six months

The medical community has finally confirmed something most parents of identical twins have always known: Our twins do not emerge from the womb purely identical. Differentiation begins when the egg splits and continues throughout their lifetimes.

Identical twins share the same DNA. This study does not dispute that. Rather, the explanation for the differences lies in epigenetics, the way identical genes that accompany that shared DNA express themselves. Genes, scientists have learned, can be turned on and off like light switches. Those switches are flipped by environmental influences. Epigenetics explains why identical twins can look somewhat different and have different inheritable diseases and conditions despite their common DNA.

I see it in my own guys.

At five years old, Matthew and Jonathan are precisely the same height. Their hands and feet are the same sizes and their hair grows in all the same directions. Yet, one is slighter than the other, overall. One has a higher-pitched voice. One has a spider vein on his face. They have different tastes in food and different levels of immunity. They are daring in different ways; shy in different ways. They are very much identical, but they are different.

Before we had Jonathan and Matthew DNA tested, when they were still infants, so many people looked for those minute differences as proof that they were fraternal. Identical twins, especially infants, should be identical in every way, they believed. It was annoying. Some of those people were relentless.

Scientists had already proven such changes take place after birth, but researchers from Murdoch Children's Research Institute (MCRI) in Melbourne are the first to prove the environment in utero can also be responsible for such changes. In the 2012 study, the Australian scientists used cord blood, placentas and umbilical cords collected at birth from both identical and non-identical twins to prove their theories, according to a recent article in the *Deccan Herald*. They found that although identical twins share the same DNA sequence, the chemical markers that switch genes on and off are different.

That makes sense to me.

In that first ultrasound at twenty weeks, the day we learned I was carrying twins, Matthew was already set to escape. He had claimed the spot at the bottom of my uterus near the cervix, the head-down position usually reserved for a baby who is prepared to make an exit. There he remained until delivery.

Jonathan seemed to spend the whole pregnancy trying to get comfortable. He was in breech position at delivery after flipping head-up and head-down a few times during the last weeks of pregnancy (That hurts, by the way!). When Matthew cleared out his space, Jonathan spent the next twenty minutes swimming, alluding the grip of my OB. He became a c-section baby when he decided to take a pike dive—head and foot first—into the world.

Their experiences in utero were entirely different. Why wouldn't that change them? What does that mean for identical siblings? For parents of identical siblings? It's hard to say. The research team believes it might help track and treat diseases earlier in life. I'm not so sure about that. I can't imagine pediatricians will suddenly start testing the cord blood of all newborns for changes in chemical markers. It's not practical.

Their team leader also noted that it might help parents understand that certain elements of fetal development are out of the parents' control. That could be comforting for some. Disconcerting for others.

For me, personally, it's a scientific answer to questions I get all the time: how can Matthew and Jonathan have physical differences and still be considered identical? It's a scientific answer for all those parents who ask on online forums how their twins might possibly be identical when their birth weights are so drastically different or they are different heights.

It's a scientific answer to support what should be common sense.

No two people will ever be precisely alike.

THE TWINS ARE READY FOR KINDERGARTEN, BUT AM I?

Five years, seven months

On September 5, Matthew and Jonathan will start kindergarten. They will be in the same classroom at our request and with the principal's blessing. He is as eager to observe the results as we are. I am nervous. I admit it. But it's not about the shared classroom.

I had always thought I'd be excited for this moment, for the moment when all four kids were in school full-time together. Same hours, same days, same vacations. One drop-off. One pick-up. It was my dream. How hard could it be, I thought. After all, the twins were in preschool four days a week last year and I was fine with that. Neither was I upset when the older kids started full-day school years ago.

But it's that fifth day that bothers me, the day I had alone with the twins. And it's those vacation days from public school that are eating away at me, the days the twins attended their private preschool and I had time alone with their older brother and sister. Those were the days we could do things that were more age-specific, things the kids could enjoy more without their older or younger siblings. Those were the days when I could let go of a little mommy-guilt and feel like I was doing as much for my children as I did when we had only two.

I'm sure I will still get time alone with each set of kids, but I'll have to work at it. Someone else—probably my husband—will have to spend time with the other two children. That limits our outings to weekends and evenings, reduces the spontaneity and limits the time we can spend together as a full family—my husband, all four kids and me. It will also make it even harder to spend alone-time with the kids individually.

I grew up in a family of eight kids. Alone-time with our parents was pretty much unheard of. I didn't suffer and I'm sure our kids won't either. Intellectually, I know that. But that doesn't make it any easier, especially in a society that insists alone time is so important for identical twins.

My husband and I already know that separation in the classroom does not equal individuality. What works is simply treating kids like individuals—all kids whether they are identical twins or whether they are a boy and a girl born seventeen months apart.

So I guess that's what I'll have to work on most.

I'll have to work harder on treating all four kids like individuals when they are together.

I can do that, right?

THEY ARE ALL YOURS, CLASS OF 2025!

Five years, seven months

Three days ago, Matthew and Jonathan started their new careers.

They are officially kindergartners.

And with their launch into the academic world has come a renewed round of the infamous question, "Are they in the same classroom?" My response ("Yes, they are.") elicits everything from raised eyebrows to pleased smiles to spontaneous lectures. I tell them the same things I have written in this blog over the past several years.

Our decision was based on recent research, conversations with identical twins and talks with teachers who have experience with twins who were placed in the same classrooms. We have the confidence that we have made the right decision, and we have the intelligence to let time, experience and Jonathan and Matthew's wishes be our guides for the future.

But, in New York State, where parents are not guaranteed a say in the placement of multiples, all the research in the world would have been irrelevant without the cooperation of an open-minded principal. Our principal has never experienced twins in the same classroom. Yet, he was fascinated by the studies we presented him and eager to do what is best for Matthew and Jonathan. So he readily agreed.

He will be watching their social and academic progress as closely as we will.

None of those concerns matter, however, to the boys. They are already having a blast and each has attached himself to a different "best friend." For the past two days, I have had to drag them out the classroom at the end of the day. My arms are weakening. I'm thinking about lining the route from the classroom to the van with freeze pops and Smarties, two of their favorite treats, to get them home.

HANDEDNESS IN IDENTICAL TWINS

In 21 percent of identical twins, one twin is right-handed and the other is either left-handed or ambidextrous, according to the folks at the Washington State Twin Registry. Since identical twins share DNA, the results provide further evidence that handedness is not genetic. Still, left-handedness occurs more frequently in twins than in singletons. Only about 10 percent of the general population is left-handed, but about 17 percent of all twins (fraternal and identical) are left-handed, studies cited by the organization show.

Matthew has always been right-handed. Jonathan started his school using different hands for different things—his right hand for drawing and his left hand for cutting; his right hand for batting and his left hand for throwing—but he has become more frequently right handed as he has aged. A handedness expert once described Jonathan as "different handed." My husband and I are both right-handed.

MY TOWERING TWINS
Five years, eight months

Silly me. I had worried that Matthew and Jonathon would be labeled by their shared DNA in school. But does anyone say, "Hey, are you the mom of the identical twins?"

No.

They say, "Hey, you're the mom of the tall twins, aren't you?"

Yes, Jonathan and Matthew have a greater claim to fame. They are off the charts for height, just like their older brother and sister, and thanks, probably, to their six-foot-five dad. I haven't measured them since July, but they were fifty inches tall then. At five years old, that puts them in the highest category, according the National Centers for Disease Control: "above the 95th percentile."

Their height has always been a problem. (They are precisely the same height, a sore subject between them.) Public tantrums were bad when they were three years old, especially since they fed off each other. But they were made worse by people who assumed they were two years older.

Once, a woman who saw one twin melting down in typical three-year-old fashion as we passed the grocery store's chip selection—a total stranger—told me I should beat him because he was too old to behave that way. (I suggested that perhaps the same discipline would be appropriate for her—the one and only time I ever managed a good comeback in the heat of the moment.)

Several times, when we visited the mall on their day off from preschool, some older woman (why the older women?) or a store clerk would demand to know (not "ask," but "demand") why they weren't in school. I admit I took pleasure in watching their nosy jaws drop when I'd say they were only four. So I knew they were taller than average and I knew their height might some-day be an issue. But, honestly, I didn't realize the difference was that great.

Few people said anything when they were in preschool. But the private preschool they attended two days a week was small and two other boys were not far behind them in height. The public preschool, where they now attend kindergarten, had a much larger class, but the kids were tucked away on one end of the building, at least during the two days the twins attended. Few people outside the preschool ever saw them.

Not so any more. Now they are in the hallways, on the playground and in the cafeteria with the rest of the elementary school crowd. Their little (still "little" to me) heads shoot up above their classmates, more on level with the first- and second-graders than with their peers. It might not seem like a handicap. People tend to reserve that stereotype for shortness. But it is.

Even when people know how old they are, it's hard to conceive. They subconsciously raise their expectations… just like I do… just like I have always done to their older brother and sister, who are also tall, despite my best efforts.

Once again though, their twinness comes to the rescue.

Rarely do they care what others think.

They have that confidence—that impenetrable space between them—that they derive from each other.

They are, as they might say, "cool with it."

TALL TWINS

Strangers who meet Jonathan and Matthew almost always assume they are a few years older than their actual ages because of their heights. When I reveal their ages, the most common response is this: "Are twins supposed to be small?"

Um, no.

Twins are often born smaller than singletons simply because of prematurity. In the case of identical twins who share a placenta in utero, the nutritional disadvantages might result in one twin being considerably smaller than the other.

Here are a few examples of some impressively tall identical twins:

Drew and Jonathan Scott, best known as HGTV's *The Property Brothers* are 6-foot-5.

Cameron and Tyler Winklevoss created the website that Mark Zuckerberg is accused of stealing to create Facebook. They are 6-foot-5.

NBA players **Robin and Brook Lopez** are 7 feet tall.

Retired WNBA stars **Heather and Heidi Burge** are 6-foot-5. They held the record as the world's tallest identical twins until they were bumped by the Recht sisters.

Former Volleyball players **Ann and Claire Recht** are in the Guinness Book of World Records as the world's tallest female twins at 6-foot-7.

IDENTICAL TWINS CAN HELP DETECT BREAST CANCER BEFORE IT DEVELOPS

Five years, eight months

Scientists practically drool over identical twins and their shared DNA, especially when one twin develops a major, and possibly genetically related illness, and the other does not. Identical twins can help unlock medical mysteries that might otherwise go unsolved.

The results of a 2012 study on breast cancer can help the rest of us appreciate the scientific fever over identical twins and their potential contributions. This is a big one.

The study, led by Manel Esteller, director of the Cancer Epigenetics and Biology Program at the Bellvitge Biomedical Research Institute (IDIBELL), Professor of Genetics at the University of Barcelona and ICREA researcher, has helped researchers identify a genetic change that occurs in those who will later develop breast cancer.

This information could lead to new blood tests that help doctors identify breast cancer victims long before their cancers actually develop. It could lead to new drugs that more efficiently target tumors and that prevent breast cancer in the first place.

It all goes back to epigenetics.

All DNA is influenced by environment. Chemical signals received by DNA can trigger certain changes, turning genes off and on like a light switch. That's the theory behind epigenetics. It's why some pairs of identical twins have clear physical differences, like height or moles or head shape. It explains lower immunity in one twin than in another. It shows why some will develop certain genetic diseases while their twins do not.

In this case, researchers found that twins with breast cancer had "a pathological gain of methylation in the DOK7 gene" years before their cancer was clinically diagnosed, according to Dr Esteller in a July 2, 2012 article on the institute's website, http://carcin.oxfordjournals.org.

The next step for the researchers will be determining the exact function of the DOK7 gene. "We believe it is a regulator of tyrosine kinases, an antitumor drug target already used for the treatment of breast cancer. If DOK7 performs this function, new studies to test drugs with tumour chemopreventive effects in breast cancer could be planned in the future," he concludes.

In simpler terms, scientists believe that a particular gene is a regulator of a drug already used to fight tumors. If that proves true, the information could lead to big changes in the way we diagnose, treat and prevent breast cancer. A simple blood test could tell women (And men. Let's not forget they can have breast cancer, too.) whether they will develop the disease in the near future.

All thanks to 36 sets of selfless identical twins.

EARLY RESULTS ARE IN: THE TWINS ARE THRIVING IN THE SAME CLASSROOM

Five years, nine months

Last week, I had our first conference with Matthew's and Jonathan's kindergarten teacher. So far, so good. Their teacher admitted he was hesitant when he learned we had requested that they be in the same classroom and, for those first few days, there were some issues. Mostly, he said, Jonathan and Matthew had to learn they could not get physical with each other in school—no poking or prodding allowed.

But now, he said, "they're just like any two kids in the classroom. When there are issues, they are just boy issues—boys being boys."

He no longer even relies on clothing to tell them apart.

Their report cards were not identical, but they were very similar. In the few areas where they differed academically, personality had a strong influence. For instance, Matthew's report card showed he could count only to 30 while Jonathan's showed a limit of 100. Matthew has been counting to 100 since he was three. It's always been a game for him and his twin brother, counting in the back seat as we drove. They also learned to count by tens at an early age. So I know he knows this stuff.

But while Jonathan sees any kind of testing as a challenge, Matthew finds it annoying. He is easily bored with reading aloud, counting and any other form of quizzing, preferring to deny knowledge so he can move on to more active pursuits. Homework with him is already a struggle.

Emotionally and socially, I saw the personality differences that have always been apparent reflected. Jonathan wears his emotions tattooed prominently across his forehead. When is angry, he is very angry. When he is sad, he is a blubbering ball of emotions.

Matthew has greater control and, though this was not on the report card, he certainly knows how to push his twin's buttons. He is emotional as well, but he is more covert—just slightly less likely to lose his cool.

Each has his own friends and a few shared ones, though they claim they are often picked on by the same girl. Our oldest daughter complains she can rarely sit with them at lunch. They usually sit at separate tables and she doesn't want to choose one over the other.

Gym class worried me the most, though.

The boys are highly competitive and they can become physically abusive to each other when they argue over games or races. But their gym teacher assured me they rarely even communicate in her class. Each goes off with his own his own group and does his own thing. Their issues in gym are more typical of their development as individuals. In the beginning, they would each get upset if they did not get the color of their choice, or if they did not get a turn. That has improved, she said, more so with one twin making bigger strides than the other (Guess who!).

A few days after the conference, I asked Matthew and Jonathan whether they enjoy being together in school and whether they might want to stay together next year.

Normally, Jonathan would begin to tear up at the thought of any separation that lasts more than a few hours, and Matthew would pounce on that, insisting they each go their own way just to a reaction. We know this because if we actually try separating them, Matthew is the first to break down.

This time, however, Matthew was the first to react positively, nodding his head vigorously.

"I want to be with my brother," he said.

"Yeah," Jonathan said, smiling. "Me, too."

SCHOOL PLACEMENT UPDATE

Both twins have anxiety issues. They are intelligent boys and it is my belief that anxiety is often a side effect of their kind of intelligence. By the end of kindergarten, we realized one twin needed time to work on his issues without impacting the other. Fortunately, our school district is tiny. We have only two classes on each grade level and their grade consists of about 34 students, total. That means the district has to get creative, combining kids of similar intellect in groups for math and reading, and sometimes placing them together for gym, recess and lunch. With the knowledge that they would spend nearly half the day together, regardless, and promises from district administrators that they could see each other whenever they needed to, the boys readily agreed to separate classrooms. It has worked out beautifully. Jonathan and Matthew see each other often throughout the day, but each has a teacher to call his own.

THANK YOU, THANK YOU, THANK YOU AND GOOD-BYE!

Six years

I'm a few days late, but I have a special gift to offer our twins for their sixth birthday.

I am officially ending this blog.

For more than five years - since they were nine months old -- I have used stories about Matthew and Jonathan to illustrate more universal issues involving identical twins. Sometimes, I've simply focused on my little guys in blog posts. Other times, I have not mentioned Jonathan and Matthew at all.

But I believe the time has come to respect their privacy.

This blog has attracted more page views than I had ever imagined possible. That tells me people crave information about identical twins whether they are raising them; involved in their care or education; or are identical twins themselves.

For that reason, I am glad that I did this.

The lack of information about raising identical twins is the force that drove me to establish this blog in the first place. I hope I have helped someone along the way by making things a little clearer, a little less frightening, a little more exciting or even just a little more interesting.

Though I will create no new posts, this blog will remain.

So if you have any questions, please comment here and I will get back to you no matter how many years have passed. Thank you so very much for reading, following and commenting. I have learned much along the way from readers, interviewees, identical siblings, and people who are simply interested in those who share DNA. Our boys have grown tremendously since I started this blog and so have we. Good-byes have always been hard for me, but here is it:

Good-bye and thank you.

It's been loads and loads of fun.

EPILOGUE

I wrote that post more than four years ago and, in looking back, I believe the timing was perfect.

I watch my boys now and I see two clearly individual human beings who love each other in ways I cannot possibly understand. They fight, but they also cry and hug when they make up. They share friends, but each has a different relationship with those friends. They often do their own thing, but when they play together, I still have to shout three times to bring them out of their shared imaginary worlds.

The fear that rattled me when I learned they were identical is gone and, I realize now, that fear dissolved around age six when they had fully and successfully managed the school environment and the social codes that come with it. School was their societal debut. We've had our challenges on that front, but they've had nothing to do with twinness.

I trust them to make their own decisions within the limits I would give any child. I trust they no longer need special guidance in dealing with issues involving their shared DNA. I trust we made good decisions when they were younger and gave them the confidence they need to grow into the amazing adults they will become.

So, I am ending this book at the same point.

Keep in mind that, at least in one sense, raising identical twins is no different than raising singletons. Children rise to expectations. If ever you are feeling overwhelmed on this special path of parenthood, think about your expectations. Adjust them if necessary and rise to them. Help your identical twins rise to them and, most important, enjoy the journey.

ACKNOWLEDGEMENTS

I would like to extend special thanks to Richard Sullivan, my former editor at *The Post-Standard*, an incredible human being and a good friend. With his critical eye and feel for language, he elevated this book to another level.

My writing friends are my rocks. Thank you to all the members of the Café – Jenny Milchman, Savannah Thorne, Lina Forrester, Sara Backer and Judy Mollen Walters. Your unending advice, your shared experiences and our weekly check-ins keep me focused when life overwhelms me. This book would not have happened without you.

Amanda Avutu, Dee Garretson and Bill McFarland, I think you all know how much you mean to me. Seven years have passed since I left our writing group and Cincinnati behind, but you three continue to inspire me with your own successes and your friendship.

Thanks you to all the readers of my blog, *The Boys: Raising Identical Twins*. (www.twinsblog.troupsburg.com). I made valuable connections, personal and professional, with readers over the years and your feedback kept me writing. You kept me sane through the craziness of twin motherhood. It is for you and because of you that I wrote this book.

And finally, my most sincere thanks go to my family. I had some pretty good freelancing gigs going and was finishing up a novel when I learned I was pregnant with twins. But I couldn't keep up the pace after they were born, not with two other young children to care for. It was getting me down. My husband, Tom Foster, came to the rescue when he suggested I start a blog. The blog became this book. Thank you, Tom, for your constant love, support and advice. I love you and am so fortunate to have you as my partner in life.

My older kids, Riley and Kiersten, have put up with a lot with a writer as a mom. I have a habit of working out murder plots while driving and blurting out some disturbing stuff. I say I have a job, but I never seem to make much money. I embarrass them with some of the passages I read out loud. Yet, they still respect my work and both are budding artists in their own rights. They are best of friends and wonderful role models for their younger brothers. I couldn't ask for more. I love you, Riley and Kiersten. Thank you.

Before I decided whether to publish this book, I asked Matthew and Jonathan for their permission. They considered it carefully and decided it was worth giving up a little of their privacy to help other parents of identical twins. That is how they think. They are amazing children. They are kind, loving, energetic, curious, funny, intelligent and empathetic. I can't imagine life without these two boys. You brighten our world. Thank you, Jonathan and Matthew, for allowing me to create and share this book. I love you both.

ABOUT THE AUTHOR

Lori Duffy Foster is a former newspaper reporter who writes fiction and nonfiction from the hills of Northern Pennsylvania, where she lives with her husband and four children. She holds a master's degree in creative writing from Binghamton University and a bachelor's degree from SUNY-Oswego. As a journalist, she covered everything from crime to education to the military for *The* (Syracuse, N.Y.) *Post-Standard*. Her short fiction has appeared in the journal *Aethlon*, and in the anthologies *Short Story America* and *Childhood Regained*. Her nonfiction has appeared in *Healthy Living*, *Running Times*, *Literary Mama*, *Crimespree* and *Mountain Home* magazines. She works on crime novels in her spare time. *Raising Identical Twins: The Unique Challenges and Joys of the Early Years* is her first published book.

Made in the USA
Middletown, DE
26 January 2021